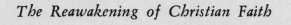

The Reawakening of Christian Faith

THE
Reawakening of
Christian Faith

BY

Bernard Eugene Meland

Essay Index Reprint Series

 BOOKS FOR LIBRARIES PRESS
FREEPORT, NEW YORK

Library of Congress Cataloging in Publication Data

Meland, Bernard Eugene, 1899–
  The reawakening of Christian faith.

  (The Clark lectures, Pomona College, Claremont,
Calif., 1947) (Essay index reprint series)
    1. Christianity––Essence, genius, nature.
I. Title. II. Series.
  ┌BR121.M46 1972┐   201'.1   72-142670
  ISBN 0-8369-2663-3

PRINTED IN THE UNITED STATES OF AMERICA
BY
NEW WORLD BOOK MANUFACTURING CO., INC.
HALLANDALE, FLORIDA 33009

THE CLARK LECTURES
Pomona College
Claremont, California
1947

Preface

THE CONVICTION HAS GROWN UPON ME IN RECENT years that the human mind struggles against almost undefeatable odds to understand its existence. It is as if one stood in a mountain pass before a distant, towering range, confident of continuing paths and slopes and hidden valleys beyond this visible façade, yet utterly unable to envision them from where he stands. Life is contained within the range of our experiences. For most of us, this means the span of sight which opens before us in any given moment. To these limited observations of our existence we can add the numerous observations of others; and, with the aid of scientific instruments, both microscopic and telescopic, our common vision can encompass far greater heights and depths of vision. So tremendous has our view of the world become through this scientific enlargement of vision that we have been content to take this view as adequate and, in fact, as representative of all existence. Empiricism, by which one means, the view of the world reported by observation and experience, has become plausible to our minds, and controlling in thought.

Yet, when we have pressed observation to these farthest limits, we are made aware of a *stop* in our existence; a horizon that blocks our view of things. This sense of a *stop* in life is made peculiarly vivid whenever the mysteries of birth and death intrude upon experience. For it is then that we realize how much we live by these observations which extend our view only to the horizon. Then we are led to say that the scientific view of life is the interim view of life. Being based on observation, it is a view shorn of mystery, of mystery that extends beyond the range of observation.

Once one is seized by the disturbing idea that reason and observation give only truncated accounts of existence, one is no longer able to be complacently empirical, nor content to remain inhospitable to imaginative efforts to comprehend the human problem in its vaster context. The great epics in poetry and in music become as a new source of sight and insight. Their affirmations of faith as well as their tragic laments take on more sobering appeal, and one realizes that all these are the heightened, and sometimes desperate, utterances of men confronting the edge of their being.

One will not relinquish the testimony of evidence that comes from experience; but one will see its limited range and relevance, and look to the testimonies of faith more wistfully.

The Christian faith becomes peculiarly intelligible when it is viewed as this inevitable reach beyond the horizons of experience to grasp for an understanding of existence which experience cannot adequately yield. Experience and faith are thus seen to be inseparable dimensions of understanding which bear the relation of tested and intuited thought.

This awakening to a new appreciation of the Christian faith is prompted, not only by a concern to enlarge our vision of the temporal span, but, more insistently, by the solicitude we all feel over the human problem because of the tragedy that stalks our path. Not that, in the face of tragedy and of overwhelming difficulty, we are justified in deserting critical thought to lapse back into the consolation of an unreflective faith; but that in confronting tragedy as a characteristic fact of experience, the human mind is routed from complacent theories, however salient, and compelled to take fresh account of the existential demands that are upon one.

No one of our generation, whatever his place or position, has escaped these disconcerting demands; for the tragedy of war and its aftermath is pervasive; and the spectre of death haunts the mind long after one has made peace with its periodic intrusions. It has been difficult for me to hold this problem of human transiency in a clear, objective light since the early years of the war, when young men in our classes began to fall in battle. When grief and resentment have subsided, we are still left with the pressing query, What does all this mean? What does life mean? In the face of our imminent dissolution, as a person or as a culture, how are we to conceive existence?

Tragedy, one might say, deepens the perspective and the tones of the human setting. Nothing is changed, in one sense; yet, in another sense, everything is radically altered. What once may have appeared in a clear light, now seems enveloped in shadows—not menacing necessarily, but with import of greater mystery. What had receded into the background, now looms with vividness, in the foreground, compelling attention. The same facts press upon our consciousness for understanding; but there is an adumbration that we had not noted before. What are these facts of existence, seen in the light of this adumbration? What is life, seen in the context of *death* and life?

The pursuit of this problem and of the importance of Christian faith as an imaginative venture in understanding our existence has steadily concerned me in recent years. When the invitation came to give The Clark Lectures at Pomona College, I seized it as an opportunity to record in brief compass what had thus far taken form in my mind and which had become compelling to me. These lectures on The Reawakening of Christian Faith are the result.

I wish to express my appreciation to President E. Wilson Lyon, of Pomona College, for inviting me to give the lectures; and to Professors Merrimom Cunniggm and John Von Rohr, of the Department of Religion in Pomona College, who undertook the work of sponsoring this occasion.

BERNARD EUGENE MELAND

Contents

xiii

CHAPTER ONE

The Nature of the Human Problem

ONE WOULD HAVE LITTLE DIFFICULTY CITING EVI-
dence that a reawakening of Christian faith has
come upon us. I am not speaking now of an awakening throughout the general culture, for I think an
impressive case could be made for saying that American culture, in substantial ways, is moving away
from Christianity. With noticeable effect, however,
and within strategic areas of our life, especially
within the thought-life of our culture, a renascent
Christian consciousness is at work.

The aftermath of war is generally marked by an
upsurge of religious interest—some of it genuine
and deep-going, resulting from an encounter with
tragedy, death, and frustration; some of it sheer
sentimental reaction; some of it formal and premed-
itated, following from a sense of timing among
calculating professionalists in religion. With all
forms of religious renascence I should not be in
sympathy, nor do I mean to endorse all in speaking
of the reawakening of Christian faith.

The return to Christianity in our time, however,

is not to be equated wholly with these post-war symptoms of reaction and resuscitation. It is a state of mind that has been with us for more than a quarter century, gradually gathering momentum until it has now reached something of a concerted tendency, especially in theological centers. In contrast to the four hundred years of human thinking dating from the late period of the Renaissance, which set up science as the arbiter of truth concerning man and his problems, this new mind-set implies a re-thinking of the fundamental concerns of life from the point of view of the Christian faith.

Such a change in perspective is of peculiar significance to the educational community; for the controlling ideas of education have been, at best, tangential to Christian thinking. The sources of insight in higher education, for example, have been, first, the humanistic tradition of the classical phase of the Renaissance; and later, with increasing momentum, the naturalistic tradition of the scientific movement dating from the time of Francis Bacon.

The tension that is often felt in the colleges between the humanities and the sciences arises from an inner conflict between these two sources of controlling ideas; and every college has the problem of resolving this tension in its educational philosophy.

Now in the midst of this educational effort, moving within the rival orbits of these two foci of the

Renaissance, the Christian tradition persists as a tempering and, occasionally, as a redirective influence. It is not controlling. The Christian tradition has never been controlling in the American colleges; for while the colleges began under Christian auspices, they conceived their educational task preeminently in the context of the humanities which derived their direction and stimulus from the Renaissance.

Yet the colleges have never been alien to the Christian tradition. In fact they have struggled valiantly to incorporate within their humanistic and science-centered enterprises the ideals of Christian living. Some have done this with more finesse and effectiveness than others. Not infrequently, however, the colleges have been forced into a self-conscious declaration of their Christian affiliation, providing periodically a religious emphasis, as it has been called, spicing up its life with a stronger salting of Christian incentive. This, in itself, has been an admission that the Christian faith is in the nature of a condiment rather than an ingredient of the educational experience.

In some respects theological liberalism eased up the problem for educators with regard to Christian influence in the colleges; for liberalism tended to divest Christianity of its theoretical compulsions. Liberalism, being itself shaped intellectually by a science-centered culture, presented Christian faith as an ethical teaching, thus reducing it to the level of practical importance. Such emphasis as came to be ascribed to religious education, social action, and moral idealism implied a Christian concern divested of theological direction on the assumption that the source of theoretical insight, in religion as in other fields of human activity, is science, not theology. And this was to say by inference that Christianity is of practical, but not of distinctive intellectual, importance. A Christianity divested of its intellectual import could thus be more readily incorporated into the educational program, centered in humanistic and scientific learning; for its impact upon the college experience was thus in the nature of a moral stimulus rather than a fundamental interpreter of thought concerning the nature of the human problem.

The crisis that is upon us in our generation derives from the fact that our confidence in the sciences and in the humanistic tradition as sources of the controlling ideas of culture and education has been visibly shaken. Our state of mind differs in this respect from that of the generation before us—say of the latter half of the nineteenth century and of the early nineteen hundreds, who confidently looked to the sciences to clarify the human problem. I do not say that this confidence in science has disappeared; for it lingers on, sustained by the momentum which it has gathered. But commitment to it as the sole and guiding truth cannot long be assured.

What obtains in the educational community has its counterpart in society at large. In modern society we are accustomed to designate business and industry as the centers of control. We have various ways of expressing this conviction: we speak of our business civilization, or of our industrial age, or of economic determinism, etc. Business and industry are controlling, however, only in the practical arena of living. Business men and industrial leaders make decisions which have their ramifications in all areas of modern life, and they control enterprises upon which the whole of our modern life depends for its sustenance—even its survival. The fact that labor has reached a stage where it can paralyze industry in seeking its ends, and, through it, the whole of society, does not alter this fact; for labor leaders are now industrial leaders, which simply means that industrial management in actuality has become dual in nature, comprising two systems of control that have yet to be resolved.

Yet, to say that industry is controlling in modern culture is to describe the situation superficially; for ideologically industry is science in action. Our industrial culture which has been steadily rising to unprecedented power and influence since, say 1840, is a thoroughgoing application of the science-centered conception of life as it has developed through technology. Thus in modern culture at large, wherever industrialization has asserted itself, the same controlling ideas appear operative as have appeared in the college and university curriculum through more than fifty years. Culture and education have been at one in conceiving the nature of the human problem to be such that an application of the findings of the sciences could ultimately, however gradually, provide a solution to our troubled lives. This presupposition, I say, is now under suspicion. In many quarters it is openly under attack.

Now it would be a mistake to regard this aroused state of mind as a frontal attack upon the sciences. Many who are of this mind are equally persuaded of the indispensable nature of science, not only in the field of action, but in certain fields of thought as well. In its basic aspect, being scientific is simply being responsive to the demands of fact. But it becomes more and more clear that our civilization in most of its aspects, including education and religion, has made such obeisance to science that it has relinquished the very outreach which can lift life above the level of sheer fact. Sheer fact cannot illumine our existence. This is the heresy that I insist upon in these lectures!

Fact gives assurance of actuality, of precision, of clarity; it does not adequately provide a full sense of reality. It does not open up to us such understanding of ourselves or of our world, of existence in all of its fullness, subtlety, and complexity, as will reveal its quality and ultimate meaning. It can give only such aid as the study of fact can reveal. This is why science is inadequate of itself to clarify the nature of the human problem.

Beyond fact is the art of imagination. Imagination without a sense for fact becomes deceptive and illusory. Concern for fact without concern for imagination issues in a barren intellectualism and in a culture for which quantity and activity are made the sole commodities of value.

In a culture dominated by the concern for fact, unattended by a restive imagination, the life of the spirit languishes. Art and music are degraded to the level of commercial entertainment or the display of talent. Religion, like business and industry, become bulk-minded, emulating rival agencies in soliciting patronage and prestige. Education becomes specialized inquiry into precise problems, essentially unrelated to the whole of life; and in this pursuit of precision and of calculable results, the quest for meaning and for the zest for life that follows upon a sense of meaning in existence, vanishes.

Our human folly that now mounts to the proportions of near catastrophe is, in no small way, directly related to our loss of stature in every realm of human thought and action, resulting from our capitulation to ends which science and industry have made sovereign—ends which can be measured only by their visible production of quantity and activity.

Stature in human existence, be it the creation of great beauty in art and music, goodness in the common life, or devotion to truth, emerges from the kind of dedication in life in which immediacies are always presented as details against the vast background of an ultimate concern. In Professor Bernard Ewer's study in Claremont, California, where I happened to be living while writing these lectures, there hangs a painting by Thompson Pritchard which would be a familiar scene to anyone living in that village. It is the depiction of sage and sand and a lone tree against a purple façade of mysterious rock, rising, so it seems, to inestimable height toward the heavens. It is in this brooding perspective in which the answerable problems of man are continuously poised against the unanswerable problems that the nature of human existence can be properly envisaged. The literature of stature, the art of stature, the education and religion of stature, have always viewed the human scene in this vaster perspective wherein man, with all his talents, achievements, and possessions, was understood in relation to his limitations; where men in their paucity of goodness, were seen in the light of their creatural possibilities; where human existence as a passing show was illumined by the outreach of the human spirit which projected this human span infinitely beyond these years that are as grass that withereth.

The modern city and village community tend to reverse this setting; for man, in his ingenuity and busyness, gathers about himself vast enterprises of his own making which he clearly understands, controls, and operates; and which he can turn to the benefit of himself in a continuous quest for physical wellbeing. And in his confidence in his handiwork, he generates a mood of cultural complacency and optimism that is in itself an insulation against the realities of existence which nevertheless play upon his life and ultimately break through to undo his impressive illusions of security and permanence.

The presuppositions of our contemporary life tend to confirm us in our illusions about existence. Education, from pre-school years to the graduate level of higher learning, attends to a fairly restricted aspect of our being, intent upon the development of skills and social adjustment. Vocation, whether in business, labor, or in the professions, narrows the range of human interest to survival and the success or failure of our varied ambitions. Society, apart from the sphere of one's work, comes to mean the arena of leisure pursuits. Even religion, as it appears in many of the churches, rarely gets beyond the conception of human existence as a truncated social experience, a round of human activity without meaning or purpose beyond the immediate sense of satisfaction which activities provide.

The church should be a threshold opening out from these immediacies of the social experience to the immensities of existence. One should enter the church as he steps through a mountain pass to envisage the panorama of events, extending the human vision illimitably beyond the moment of living. But alas, more often the church is a continuation of this endless round of affairs, confirming its members, already insulated from the issues of existence, in their social complacency and trivial pursuits. The churches could rescue men and women from their ignominy as mere social animals and awaken them to greater stature as creatures of the living God; but they, too, have become immersed in the presuppositions of the contemporary culture which precludes their seeing beyond the weekly calendar of events. Hartley Burr Alexander, who was one of the wisest men of our generation, wrote in his *Truth and the Faith,* "As for the Protestant Churches, none shows sign of a vitality that is more than may be generated by the gregarious warmth of little

communities: for where are they open to the great-
ness of the skies?"

The insistent demand upon the sensitive mind
today, which tries to fathom the source and nature
of our predicament as modern men and women, is
to recover this vision of the human scene which
gives the full meaning of our human problem, making apparent also the limitations under which we
live as human creatures. It is this insistence to adequately understand the nature of the human problem, more than any other stimulus, that presses for
an awakening of Christian faith in our time.

II

The readiness to regard this renewed interest in
Christian faith as reactionary thinking needs to be
questioned and appraised. It is quite common to
designate this new Christian emphasis "neo-orthodoxy," and thus to dismiss it as a threat to liberalism.
Actually there are only two clear expressions of
neo-orthodoxy in modern theological thought in
the sense that solution to our modern human problem is sought in the re-creation of some ancient
system of thought. One is the Neo-Thomist philosophy which has given new life to Roman Catholic
institutions; the other is the Neo-Reformation
theology, particularly as it appears in the writings

of Karl Barth, notably in his *Dogmatics*. Somewhat within the orbit of Barth's influence are to be found such varying thinkers as Emil Brunner, Paul Tillich, and Reinhold Niebuhr. Of these, only Brunner could be called a disciple of Barth; and their divergence is indicated by the quip which runs, When Brunner says *"Jah!"*, Karl Barth can be counted on to say, *"Nein!"* and vice versa. It is well to remember, however, that people nearest together disagree. Where they are oceans apart in their thinking they cannot even converse; and usually they do not.

Reinhold Niebuhr is our most eminent American representative of theological reaction. His influence has done more in the past two decades to dissipate the hold of theological liberalism on the American pulpit than that of any other voice. His book, *Reflections on the End of an Era*, published in 1934, might well be considered the marking of the end of an era in American religious thought, for since its publication, the emergence of a new theological mood in our time has been mounting, becoming more and more pervasive. Certainly it would be a mistake to speak of Reinhold Niebuhr as an exponent of neo-orthodoxy, except in the most general sense. For while he revives the imagery of thought familiar to orthodox Christian thinkers, his analysis of modern man and of the follies of modern culture is clearly in the modern mode. His most effective source of insight, by which he penetrates the illusions and self-pride of modern man, is depth psychology, not ancient theology; though it is through the study of depth psychology that Niebuhr is led to reaffirm the Christian appraisal of man and to insist upon the familiar, theological premise that man cannot be understood apart from reflection upon his relation to God. In this re-orientation of man, the nature of the human problem is re-defined. It is no longer the problem of extending the human enterprise through the pursuit of rational inquiry, or the social application of moral idealism. These, Niebuhr regards as paths of delusion which brought liberalism to a dead-end in a religion of self-worship. Seen in relation to the God of the Christian faith, he argues, the problem of man is himself—not his bestiality, necessarily, as the liberal was prone to contend,[1] but his humanity, his moralisms and his intellectual pride, his tendency to think more highly of himself than he ought to think. This reversal of the spiritual equation, designating man at his best the worst offence against God because it issues in self-love and idolatry, makes Niebuhr's thought completely antithetical to the liberal's gospel.

To understand how Niebuhr comes to this para-

---

[1] The liberal's use of the theory of evolution led to his equating sin with man's bestiality. Cf. S. Mathews, *The Gospel and the Modern Man.* New York, Macmillan, 1910; and W. Rauschenbusch, *Christianizing the Social Order.* New York, Macmillan, 1912.

doxical analysis of the condition of man, we may look to some of the sources of his thought. Clearly, the positive sources of his thinking are to be found in certain strains of historic theology such as St. Paul, Augustine, and Calvin. The more immediately formative influences are Kierkegaard and certain strains of modern existentialism, particularly that of Heidigger and Max Scheler.

It is safe to say that Kierkegaard's *The Concept of Dread*,[2] is the most informing source of Niebuhr's thinking on sin. It is here, in fact, that one gets the fullest amplification of the idea of anxiety being the basic condition out of whch sin arises. Anxiety, says Kierkegaard, results from the *dizziness of freedom* —the opening up before one of the panorama of yet unrealized possibilities of the human situation as seen from the point of view of his ultimate destiny, accompanied by a consciousness of his fixities, being himself a creature of nature. It is in this existential situation, says Niebuhr, that man must act; he must make decisions.[3] These transactions and decisions in which freedom is exercised in the context of contingency is history. Man, as spirit, creates history. Man as mind and body can be subsumed under nature and can pursue a course that seeks only accom-

2 *Der Begriff der Angst*. Trans. by Lowrie. Princeton, Princeton University Press, 1944.
3 *The Nature and Destiny of Man*, Vol. I. New York, Scribner's, 1941, pp. 162f.

modation to natural demands. The spiritual end of man demands that he do more than this; that he pitch his life toward the level of history, from which he may rise to the further level of decision as impelled by the Kingdom of God—a realm of meaning beyond history in the sense that history is beyond nature.

Now this is the context in which sin takes on meaning for Niebuhr. This precarious predicament of being in history poised, as it were, between possibilities of rising to the demands of God's kingdom and of exploiting our transcendent capacities for lesser ends—ourselves, provides the arena of sin. Our possibilities confound us. Unlike the Christ, confronting the temptation of power and possession, we fall; not through decision, but through the dizziness that takes hold of us, placed as we are on so high a pinnacle. In our dizziness we become anxious; and in our anxiety, we lose sight of the possibilities that are in God. We no longer look up, but down at the terrifying folly that could befall us. In our fear of tumbling from these heights, we clutch at whatever will give security. Man, obsessed with the concern for security, is no longer dedicated to the high good. He cannot be. What man does to achieve a sense of security in this condition of anxiety, magnifies his sinful state; for this may take a deceptive turn that leads to actual rebellion against

God. Man's fear is then concealed beneath a parade of arrogance. Man stands constantly in this ambiguous predicament of possibility and contingency —of seeing a kingdom of spirit opening up before him, yet feeling simultaneously the demands of his own life, bent on security.

The human problem that is paramount, then, is always the inversion of spirit that takes place in man—of turning that which is a spiritual capacity into willful rebellion against God. The good that is in man, though it is to be acknowledged, is not to be accounted good; for this is the source of his demonry. Extending that good will give no assurance of bettering the world or of saving man; for the issue of destruction lies concealed here.

In Niebuhr's conception of man and of the human problem, therefore, we see the whole course of thinking and of social planning that was pursued in theological liberalism and in modern idealism reversed. For the supporting ideology is reversed. Instead of immanentism that permitted of a ready identification of human value with divine value, Niebuhr insists upon a transcendent view of God that places human value in suspect. Instead of reliance upon rationality as man's most dependable instrument for effecting his social salvation, Niebuhr points to the illusions of rationality. Instead of the creed of meliorism, the conviction that the world is getting progressively better, Niebuhr relinquishes every remnant of hope in human progress. Man's hope is in the depth of his hopelessness that will bestir him to take a proper measure of himself—that will impel him not to think more highly of himself than he ought to think. Restraint of pride and of the illusion of self-righteousness, he admonishes, can provide us with realism to confront the human problem with a sober realization of the plight we are in and of the magnitude of our sin. The despair that may follow will make possible "the contrition which appropriates the divine forgiveness. It is in this contrition and in the appropriation of divine mercy and forgiveness," Niebuhr writes, "that the human situation is fully understood and overcome." [4]

Man, then, says Niebuhr, will not solve his problem, as the modern man is inclined to assume; nor will history; for ultimately the solution is the redemption of man. And this is the work, not of men, but of God.

A name which is not commonly associated with the reaction against theological liberalism is that of Henry Nelson Wieman. Yet Wieman's thought has made as spirited an attack upon liberalism and modern idealism as the theology of Barth and Niebuhr,

[4] *The Nature and Destiny of Man.* New York, Scribner's, 1943, Vol. II, pp. 56–57.

and may properly be considered, in this respect, an expression of theological reaction. His denunciation of *the religion of illusion* in his early writings, directed chiefly, no doubt, against all popular forms of evangelical religion that sentimentalized faith, was levelled also against every subjective procedure in religion that appealed to feeling and to idealization in disregard of fact.

The religion of illusion (he wrote), this religion of sugar and spice and all things nice, must be fought as we fight the White Plague and the Black Death.[5]

A defensible religion, he continued:

insists that facts are more important than any cherished mistaken beliefs, no matter how unpleasant the facts and how delightful the beliefs. It insists that this is not a nice world and God is not a nice God. God is too awful and terrible, too destructive to our foolish little plans, to be nice. But God is a fact and this world is made up of facts; and if we are ever to live securely and magnificently in this world (or any other) it can only be through adaptation to these facts.[6]

Wieman advanced his criticism, not only against theological liberalism that rested its case upon the appeal to religious experience, but against all forms of mysticism that set up intuition as a special form of knowledge, and against philosophical idealism,

[5] From H. N. Wieman: *The Wrestle of Religion with Truth*. Copyright, 1927 by The Macmillan Company and used with their permission.
[6] *Ibid.*, p. 3.

both in its speculative use of reason, unsupported by empirical evidence, and in its appeal to ideals as guides to human conduct. His repudiation of devotion to ideals is strikingly akin to Niebuhr's strictures on self-love. Wieman writes:

> There is today a widespread tendency to identify religion with devotion to ideals . . . Is religion preeminently a device for glorifying social cooperation and arousing utmost devotion to those goals of endeavor which society holds to be highest? . . Or is it the reconstruction of ideals? . . We are very sure that the greatest obstacle in the way of individual growth and social progress is the ideal which dominates the individual or the group . . . Our ideals have in them all the error, all the impracticability, all the perversity and confusion that human beings who are themselves erring, impracticable, perverse and confused, can put into them. Our ideals are no doubt the best we have in the way of our constructions. But the best we have is pitifully inadequate.[7]

Every tendency to identify religion or God with human ideals or values drew from Wieman a sharp rebuff. He was critical of the functional effort of Ames to equate God with our highest social values as well as of the avowed commitment to man in religious humanism. It was, in fact, the tendency in liberalism toward a man-centered faith that evoked his strictures upon its subjectiveness. Wieman saw

[7] From H. N. Wieman: *Religious Experience and Scientific Method.* Copyright, 1926 by The Macmillan Company and used with their permission, pp. 267–268.

what Barth had learned from Feuerbach, that the logical outcome of the subjective appeal in liberalism was humanism. And humanism meant to Wieman the relinquishment of man's reach toward what is ultimately saving and fulfilling. Man cannot save himself, he insisted.

What obscured Wieman's critical reaction against liberalism was his insistent appeal to scientific method. To him science, by which he meant cooperative inquiry, provided the only empirical alternative to revelation. Tested knowledge, such as emerged from cooperative inquiry, he contended, did not carry the limitation which he, along with Niebuhr and Barth, attributed to human reason and subjective experience. In cooperative inquiry one was guarding against the unconscious drives and compulsions that colored and corrupted all subjective thinking. To this extent there was transcendence of the human ego, yielding an objective, disinterested knowledge in religion which gave assurance that its basis was fact, not mere feeling or wishful thinking. Wieman saw the limited range to which this method of thinking could be applied in the religious field, but he regarded this minimum degree of certainty as all important. It was, he thought, the sole source of assurance that what one appeals to as the sovereign good, is actually good in an ultimate sense; actually man's saving good.

Confident that he had come upon a procedure for discerning the action of God as an empirical event, Wieman has been led to look at Christian history normatively, concerned to distinguish in these records between what actually reveals God at work in history and what was simply the report of men's feelings and unfounded hopes.[8] The Christian faith, thus clarified, is for him the historic witness to the structure of events that has been, is now, and will forever be creative of good.

Wieman's return to an emphasis upon the Christian faith must be interpreted somewhat differently from that of neo-orthodoxy or Neo-Reformation theologians; for, quite obviously, the fulcrum of his thought is the criterion which his philosophy of religion defines as creative good. It would be inaccurate, however, simply to say that his philosophy of religion has been made a substitute for the historic faith. Rather, as he intends it, his criterion is the intellectual tool by which the actual saving good, disclosed in history, and to which the Christian faith bears witness, may be isolated, set apart from the illusory creations of human imagination and feeling. The risk of iconoclasm here is grave; but Wieman's sense for fact outweighs all other considerations in his thinking. He prefers this risk

[8] *The Source of Human Good.* Chicago, University of Chicago Press, 1946, chapter X.

to the risk of illusion, which he regards the more deadly error.

III

The burden of this reawakened Christian consciousness, however, must be seen as something more than a theological argument. It is, in fact, a cultural revolution that reaches into every appraisal of the human spirit. This re-evaluation of the human spirit is vividly exemplified in the reactionary outlook and mood among literary minds and critics. One can speak of this phase with some justification as the literary roots of theological reaction for, in important respects, it was prior to the theological change in thought.

Changes in critical perspectives began to occur in Europe before they became manifest in this country. The book *Speculations*, by T. E. Hulme, a series of essays in art criticism written before the first world war, but published later, had begun to throw the influence of art and literature in England on the side of the doctrine of discontinuity and to urge the end of facile liberal hopes in religion. Nothing comparable to Hulme's book spoke out of the American experience until Joseph Wood Krutch's *The Modern Temper*, which appeared as the depression was reaching its depth in 1929. The difference between these two books was one of illumination. Krutch's *Modern Temper* was a lament with no hint of salvation, while Hulme's book sought to advance thought constructively and with imagination toward a new supernaturalism.

Quite unwittingly, I think, the free verse revolt in poetry, which had been initiated by Ezra Pound, provided a reactionary stimulus in the form of a neo-classicism, not unrelated to the efforts of Hulme. The writings of T. S. Eliot were to give to this neo-classical trend its decisive theological turn and to make of it an impressive voice in behalf of tradition.

T. S. Eliot published *The Wasteland* in 1922. Having lived in London since 1914, Eliot was really a British, rather than an American voice. Yet his influence has been felt among us wherever criticism has reached a religious depth. *The Wasteland* is generally regarded as "the closing poem of the romantic era in British and American poetry." [9] It was, in any case, a decisive voice of despair, disillusioned with western thinking and with western, democratic institutions. Kreymborg writes in *Our Singing Strength*, An Outline of American Poetry:

The Eliot regime is based on the general disillusionment of the World War aftermath. Eliot adopted the aristocracy of the

[9] Alfred Kreymborg, *Our Singing Strength*, An Outline of American Poetry (1620–1930). New York, Coward McCann, 1929. With permission of the publishers.

intellect over the cruder emotions, conscious, however, of the fact that the world is ruled, not by the integrity of intelligence, but by the brute instincts, marvelously developed, of men who rule the mass of people politically. The fact that these men are elected by the people adds to the poet's disdain, forces him deeper into himself, and has made his aristocratic art a thing of complete despair. And despair is the keynote of the latest generation.[10]

If despair with the modern individual consciousness and its institutions is a motivating force in Eliot's writing, recovery of the sense of tradition, by which the limitations of the individual consciousness are overcome, marks the affirming note of his thought. Eliot took up the battle of discontinuity where T. E. Hulme had staked it out in *Speculations*. In the opening chapter of the book *Revelation*,[11] Eliot has this telling sentence: "The division between those who accept, and those who deny, the Christian revelation I take to be the most profound division between human beings." This division, he goes on to say, not only goes deeper than divisions of political faith, of class or race; but it is different in kind. The two cannot be measured by the same scale.[12]

[10] *Ibid.*, 526.
[11] Edited by Baillie and Martin. New York, Macmillan, 1937.
[12] *Ibid.*, p. 2.

Eliot found refuge from the despair of his *Waste-land* in the Anglo-Catholic faith, and his subsequent writings, as in poems like *The Rock,* and *Ash Wednesday,* and in essays such as *The Sacred Wood, After Strange Gods* and *Essays Ancient and Modern, The Idea of a Christian Society,* he has persistently declared this faith.

As early as 1916, Edwin Arlington Robinson had delineated the tragic vision of the human scene in his "Man Against the Sky." [13]

> Whatever the dark road he may have taken,
> This man who stood on high
> And faced alone the sky,
> Whatever drove or lured or guided him, . . .
> His way was even as ours;
> And we, with all our wounds and all our powers,
> Must each await alone at his own height
> Another darkness or another light; . . .
> Are we no greater than the noise we make
> Along one blind atomic pilgrimage
> Whereon by crass chance billeted we go
> Because our brains and bones and cartilage
> Will have it so?
> If this we say, then let us all be still
> About our share in it, and live and die
> More quietly thereby.[14]

[13] New York, Macmillan, 1916.
[14] From Robinson: *Man Against the Sky.* Copyright, 1916 by Edwin Arlington Robinson. Used by permission of The Macmillan Company.

With this, his sensitive mind could not be content.
And so the query came again:

Where was he going, this man against the sky?
You know not, nor do I.
But this we know, if we know anything:
That we may laugh and fight and sing
And of our transcience here make offering
To an orient Word that will not be erased,
Or, save in incommunicable gleams
Too permanent for dreams,
Be found or known.
No tonic and ambitious irritant
Of increase or of want
Has made an otherwise insensate waste
Of ages overthrown
A ruthless, veiled, implacable foretaste
Of other ages that are still to be
Depleted and rewarded variously
Because a few, by fate's economy,
Shall seem to move the world the way it goes.
.   .   .   .
No planetary trap where souls are wrought
For nothing but the sake of being caught
And sent again to nothing will attune
Itself to any key of any reason
Why man should hunger through another season
To find out why 'twere better late than soon
To go away and let the sun and moon
And all the silly stars illuminate
A place for creeping things. . . . .
If after all that we have lived and thought,

All comes to Nought,——
And we be nothing anyhow,
And we know that,—why live?
'Twere sure but weaklings' vain distress
To suffer dungeons where so many doors
Will open on the cold eternal shores
That look sheer down
To the dark tideless floods of Nothingness
Where all who know may drown.[15]

To rise to this stubborn discontent with life's transciency was at least to get a footing upon the boulders against whose sleek, wet granite incessant waves of pessimism lashed their spray. Robinson never got beyond this haunting recognition of the tragic sense of life. His last work, *King Jasper*,[16] was his darkest, and left little to which even the most sanguine might look forward. One might almost believe that he foresaw the debacle of these recent years.

Robinson Jeffers [17] is, in his own way, a stronger voice than either Robinson or Eliot; for while he shares Robinson's bitterness and lament and Eliot's cold disdain; he rises above the pitying mood to say with a certain Calvinistic arrogance:

---

[15] *Man Against the Sky.*
[16] New York, Macmillan, 1935.
[17] Especially his narrative poems, *Roan Stallion*. New York, Horace Liveright, 1925; *Tamar* (in *Roan Stallion*); *The Women At Point Sur*, New York, Random House, 1927; *Dear Judas*. New York, Horace Liveright, 1929; and *Such Counsels You Gave To Me*. Random House, 1937.

We have granite and cypress,
Both long lasting,
Planted in the earth. . . . .
We wonder why tree tops
And people are so shaken.[18]

If this were just a Californian's cool equanimity from living in isolation above the crags and cypresses on the Carmel Coast, it would have little relevance here. But in Robinson Jeffers we have the modern poet recapturing something of American Calvinism as it was once expressed in Jonathan Edwards.[19] Between Jonathan Edwards and Robinson Jeffers lie three centuries of thought. Meanwhile the concepts of the sciences have crept in to replace theological concepts. Nevertheless, Robinson Jeffers would have listened with understanding and approval to Edwards' sermons; and when Edwards shouted, "Are you willing to be damned for the glory of God?" Jeffers would have replied, in whispers that only he, himself, could have heard, "I am willing. I give my heart to the hawks!" And by the same token, if Jonathan Edwards, were he to be aroused from whatever company he now keeps, and brought back again to the American earth, could

[18] From "Granite and Cypress" in *Roan Stallion*. Used by permission of the author.
[19] Cf. F. Carpenter, "Value in Robinson Jeffers," *American Literature*, Vol. 11, p. 357. See also "The Radicalism of Jonathan Edwards," by F. Carpenter, *New England Quarterly*, IV, 637–639.

read *Roan Stallion,* or *The Women at Point Sur,* he would say, "A strange character, this fellow Jeffers. His language is strange; but his ideas are sound. Jeffers' ideas are sound."

Jeffers, moved by the self-same disillusionment that sent Eliot to England and into Anglo-Catholicism, reached back into his ancestry and found the Calvinist vein in his own nature. Jeffers', quite obviously, is no pure reactionary mind. He brings to poetry the realism of modern science.[20] Yet, for all his scientific vocabulary and his Freudian perceptions, the emotional tone, and, to a considerable degree, the imagery itself, when applied to man's estate, betrays his Calvinistic feeling, however masqued.[21]

His fierce feeling for objectivity when he is declaring his major theme:

> Integrity is wholeness,
>
> .   .   .   .
>
> Love that, not man apart from that, or else
>   you will share man's pitiful confusions,
>   or drown in despair when his days darken.[22]

has in it the note of adoration that affirms "divine

---

[20] Cf. H. H. Waggoner, "Science and the Poetry of Robinson Jeffers," *American Literature,* Vol. 10, pp. 275ff.

[21] J. S. Fletcher, "The Dilemma of Robinson Jeffers," *Poetry,* 43: pp. 338ff.

[22] From "The Answer" in *Such Counsels You Gave to Me,* p. 107. Used by permission of the author.

beauty" for its own sake. And his disdain for the
corruptness of man, bespeaking neither the influence of science nor the appeal of monistic mysticism,
recalls the vehemence of a Jonathan Edwards, de-
crying the condition of man.

> What is man? The filthiest of beasts;
> But a discoverer.[23]

The full import of Jeffers' thought as a force of
reaction is to be found in this repetitious exposé of
man's corruptness and of *the humanist's tragedy*.
Man, of himself, is both corrupt and futile.

> The only animal that turns means
> to an end. What end? Oh, but what end? [24]

To love man, as W. S. Johnson has paraphrased
Jeffers' words, "is to love the abnormal, the corrupt,
the ephemeral." [25]
The idealism that had impelled the social liberal
to crusade for a better world, or that had inspired
the humanist to sing his praise of man, evokes from
Jeffers his bitterest rebuke:

Humanity is the mold to break away from, the crust to

[23] *The Women At Point Sur*, p. 34.
[24] "The Humanist's Tragedy," in *Dear Judas*, p. 123.
[25] W. S. Johnson, "The 'Savior' in the Poetry of Robinson Jeffers."
American Literature, Vol. 15, pp. 159ff.

break through, the coal to break into fire, The atom to be split.[26]

But even if our humanity were a cause to advance, we could not advance it as the social liberal and the humanist so desperately intended:

Why do we invite the world's rancors and agonies
Into our minds though walking in a wilderness? Why did he
want the news of the world? He could do nothing
To help nor hinder. Nor you nor I can . . for the world.
It is certain the world cannot be stopped nor saved.
It has changes to accomplish and must creep through agonies
toward new discovery. It must, and it ought: the awful
necessity
Is also the sacrificial duty. Man's world is a tragic music and
is not played for man's happiness,
Its discords are not resolved but by other discords.
But for each man
There is real solution, let him turn from himself and man
to love God. He is out of the trap then. He will remain
Part of the music, but will hear it as the players hear it.
He will be superior to death and fortune, unmoved by success
or failure. Pity can make him weep still,
Or pain convulse him, but not to the center, and he can conquer them . . But how could I impart this knowledge
To that old man? [27]

I will mention one more poet in pointing up this background of despair that has routed liberalism:

[26] *Roan Stallion,* p. 20.
[27] From "Going To Horse Flats," in *Such Counsels You Gave to Me,* pp. 90–91. Used by permission of the author.

Edna St. Vincent Millay.[28] If, as Allen Tate says in his *Reactionary Essays*,[29] Millay is not an intellect, but a sensibility, she must nevertheless be credited with having influenced some of the most acute intellects among our younger preachers, who, like the late Ted Hume, brought, to the intellectual diet of Reinhold Niebuhr, the lyrical support of Edna St. Vincent Millay's lyrics and sonnets which spoke so poignantly of *the mind's allegiance to despair.*

Between the mood of despair and the attitude of faith, as the reactionary mind of our time has embraced it, there is but a small, transitional passage— a bridge across a moat, one might say, precariously flung across uncertain waters. Faith, Brunner has said, follows upon the full realization of despair. "Only the soul that despairs knows what it means to believe, and faith teaches to despair rightly." [30] The transition to a new found faith was provided for the young theological mind, in many instances, by poetry that winsomely inveigled them into despair.

Not that for the poet, faith was a visible consequence; on the contrary, poets like Millay could

---

[28] Especially *Fatal Interview.* New York, Harper, 1931; *Wine From These Grapes.* New York, Harper, 1934; and *Conversation At Midnight.* New York, Harper, 1937.

[29] New York, Scribner's, 1936.

[30] Emil Brunner, *The Mediator.* Philadelphia, Westminster Press, 1947, p. 151.

rest back upon a hedonism that gives to despair an aesthetic resolution. The fate of man

> who when his destiny was high
> Strode like the sun into the middle sky
> And shone an hour, and who so bright as he,
> And like the sun went down into the sea,
> Leaving no spark to be remembered by.[31]

bringing to naught the high ventures of man's proud intellect and his moral endeavor, only argues to the hedonist that man, with his *animal heart,* can wrest his plight from ignominy by becoming sensible to beauty and its loves. If Millay points to Donne and to Kierkegaard, she, herself, returns again and again, in her own resolution of the human plight, to Baudelaire and to John Cowper Powys.

Now I have come around through this by-path of literary citation, in part, because I see these literary figures as our most eloquent spokesmen for the mood that has urged upon us a new theological approach to the human problem; but even more because each one of these figures calls to mind some young preacher, theologian, or philosopher, who, in the process of seeking his way out of the chaos of his disillusioned liberalism, followed the beckon-

---

[31] From Sonnet IV of "Epitaph For The Race of Man" in *Wine From These Grapes,* p. 64. Published by Harper & Brothers. Copyright, 1928, by Edna St. Vincent Millay.

ing of one of these alluring voices, and along their path, found his way either into a new supernatural-ism, or, as in some cases, into a more realistic road beyond liberalism leading toward a religious nat-uralism.

The transition from any one of these voices of despair to Kierkegaard, thence to Barth or Niebuhr is a natural one. I would say it is even inevitable for the theologian who needs more than lyrical senti-ment to sustain his reaction in thought; unless he should turn to neo-Thomism or to the Anglican church, as, apparently many of our literary people have done.[32]

IV

All roads beyond liberalism, however, do not lead back to some new form of orthodoxy. There are in-stances of reaction leading to a more discerning religious naturalism.[33] This may be the place to point in a direction where fresh illumination on the human problem is emerging, presaging rapport with the Christian Faith.

To find a name suitable for designating this vast new complex of insight on the horizon which tow-

[32] See Bernard Iddings Bell, "Those Who Came Back," *Atlantic Monthly.* Also, *The Church in Disrepute*, New York, Harper, 1943.

[33] Cf. Benjamin Miller, "Mythological Naturalism," *Journal of Religion*, XXII, 270–287. July, 1942.

ers before us like new accumulations of the mind, would be somewhat taxing. I shall not attempt to name it. It does not have the distinctiveness of a movement of thought, for its perspective has been pervasive in many fields of thought; and while it has been gaining steadily in force for over two decades, its advances have been almost imperceptible. To enumerate all of the fields in which it has been shaping thought would be tedious. It would include instances from such diverse areas as the new physics, dating from Becquerel and Rutherford, from *Gestalt* psychology initiated by Wertheimer, the new metaphysics issuing from Bergson through Whitehead, the philosophy of religion of Wieman and Hartshorne, and the cultural engineering of Lewis Mumford.

What is common here is a fresh awareness of the concept of relations which has greatly extended and widened the meaning of existence. In contrast to the full-orbed reality envisaged here, the oversimplified setting in which pragmatic liberalism conceived the human problem seems an arbitrary and restricted sphere of social experience, extricated from the total picture in a way that scientific method must always extricate its data.

Now it must not be assumed that all of these areas of thought in which horizons have been pushed back and the sense of connections established, contribute to the Christian awakening we have been describing. All I mean to imply is that the release from a restrictive, sociological orientation of thought has given rise to a new intellectual climate, which may provide the stimulus and the ground for advancing beyond theological reaction and sheer existentialism where the only alternatives can be irrational faith, as in Barthianism, or irrational despair, as in the French existentialism of Sartre.

The disturbing fact is that, despite the pervasive influence of its controlling concept, the perspective itself has not been formative beyond philosophy and the sciences. With the possible exception of the work of Lewis Mumford, no literary figure has been moved to explore its imaginative implications in the sense that Dante was gripped by scholasticism; or that Shelley and Wordsworth and Swinburne were informed by Romanticism; or that certain contemporary writers have been seized by the current reactionary passion. This may be because the full force of its organizing ideas has not as yet been felt beyond the most technical areas of thought.

In the form in which this perspective has appeared in these technical areas, it has not elicited sharp reaction, on the one hand, nor dramatic commitment, on the other. Being in the nature of a constructive force, it is not combative; conse-

quently it does not invite discursive champions.
Wherever its categories are incorporated, they effect an integrating experience. Facts, in their new
context, are not radically changed; they are simply
given more depth and perspective by reason of a
new sense of relations. Fragments are formed into a
whole. Separate entities are brought into a unity.
Individuals are made sensible of the community.

The integration that has here become formative
in thought and experience is not to be confused
with mechanism where the whole is the sum of its
parts; nor with that kind of synthesis that was implied in Hegelianism where the whole absorbed all
of its parts into its absolute category. It is the nature
of relations to be dynamic, interactive, creative. In
this contextualism the parts remain creative centers
of influence while the patterns of meanings that result from their interrelationship give genuinely new
dimensions of insight and power.

The force of this perspective has been minimized,
no doubt, beyond the technical areas in which it has
been formative, by the very fact that it has been
essentially constructive in its effect upon thought.
Creativeness is neither as evident nor as exciting as
combat or destruction. Growth occurs unobserved;
destruction arouses a multitude. The happenings
that have been shaping human thought toward a
new conception of man and his problems are too

numerous to recount, but they could be designated. Simply designating them, however, would not suggest the full stature of this movement of thought which has been in the nature of a groundswell—so gradual and extensive in scope and influence that it has often been imperceptible. Looking back over several centuries of thought, as Whitehead did in *Science and the Modern World* [34] or as Boodin did in his *Three Interpretations of the Universe;* [35] or compressing the picture within the span of fifty years, as Lewis Mumford did in one section of his *Technics and Civilization,* [36] one finds that a revolution in fundamental notions has visibly taken place. Superficially, what one sees is that the presuppositions which once bolstered the mechanistic outlook of materialism or of historic naturalism and which sanctioned positivism and its descendants, have been relinquished. A new spirit moves among both profound and technical thinkers in all fields, impelling them to become more discerning of that which is unaccounted for in any quantitative description of events—the *more* in existence and in man's nature which prompts one to speak of spirit.

So far the new mysteriousness that attends this new vision of science and of philosophy has served largely an apologetic purpose in theology and reli-

[34] New York, Macmillan, 1925.
[35] New York, Macmillan, 1934.
[36] New York, Harcourt and Brace, 1934, pp. 368ff.

gion, reinforcing, sometimes in sentimental ways, beliefs or inclinations already held on habit. The exception has been the careful and persistent work of men like Charles Hartshorne and Henry Nelson Wieman who, while differing sharply in their views, nevertheless pursue their separate ends within a common perspective that takes account of this new vision in the sciences.[37]

Hartshorne combines the gifts of the rationalist with a sound sense for the importance of feeling. In this respect he emulates Spinoza and Whitehead. He is thus able to bring sharpened intellectual tools to the task of analyzing and clarifying familiar, though vague, religious ideas which have suffered from sentimentalization and which, because they have had little more than a basis in feeling, have been ignored or neglected in disciplined thought. Such is the idea of God as love or as providence. Utilizing the notion of *internal relations*, which Whitehead developed in *Process and Reality*, Hartshorne has made an impressive case for the rational necessity of theistic providence, designating God the inescapable companion.[38] Another such idea is the immortality of good. Hartshorne is quite explicit in his rejection of the idea of individual immortality; not only, as

[37] See Hartshorne's article, "The Theological Values in Current Metaphysics," *Journal of Religion*, Vol. 26: 157–167.
[38] *Man's Vision of God*. Chicago, Willett, Clark, 1941.

he contends, for lack of evidence, but for lack of a moral defence of the idea, itself. Yet he regards the persistence of the values which give meaning to our existence as a basically rational idea. He writes:

It has often been said that immortal life is now, and is a quality, not a mere quantitative extension of living. But what this means, who of the older schools of theology has told us? Yet the social view of reality and of God can tell us. Each of us is, in his very being, his very life just as lived on earth, a contribution to the experience of God. This experience is indestructible; for in order to take on new content God has no need to forget the old . . We contribute once for all, every moment, our very being of that moment to the undying treasury of all good.[39]

Perhaps the force of Hartshorne's work comes, not so much from the clean, logical clarity of his thought (although that gives to his analyses a chaste quality that is literary in style) as from his complete assimilation of the multiple stimuli that have converged toward a new theism. The surety that he conveys, for example, in characterizing the inadequacy of humanism derives from a clear grasp of the evidences from the sciences as well as of the philosophical reasons that reinforce his criticisms.[40]

Hartshorne has already given some attention to

---

[39] "Theological Values in Current Metaphysics," *op. cit.*, p. 167.
[40] See his *Beyond Humanism*, especially Part I.

the encyclopedic task of correlating the significant advances in metaphysics as they bear upon the theological concern,[41] but he is qualified, both by ability and interest, to wrest, from the converging intellectual accumulations in philosophy and in science, the structural ideas that will inform and fortify theology in its constructive task.

The constructive phase of Mr. Wieman's work has centered almost exclusively around the problem of value.[42] For Wieman, defining the structure of value that is worthy of the designation, "Good" is tantamount to defining God. I say tantamount, because Wieman does not mean to say that the meaning of God is exhausted by a structure of events. He is concerned to say, however that God's work in any situation is discernible because it has a character that is describable. Wherever God is at work, new perspective emerges and becomes integrated with the old, resulting in a widening of appreciative awareness and a deepening of community. This fourfold happening is the creative event that makes for enduring goodness. When men give them-

---

[41] "Theological Values in Current Metaphysics," *op. cit.*

[42] Beginning with his essay "God and Value," in *Religious Realism* by D. C. Macintosh, et al., New York, Macmillan, 1931, he pursued a consistent course of defining and redefining value as a criterion for designating God. See also *Normative Psychology of Religion* (with R. W. Wieman) New York, Crowell, 1935; "Values: Primary Data For Religious Inquiry," *Journal of Religion*, Vol. 16: pp. 379–405, Oct. 1936; *The Source of Human Good*. Chicago, University of Chicago Press, 1946.

selves in utter devotion to this creativity they are serving the highest and ultimate good. Wieman believes that this structure of events is discernible in the records that report events following the coming of the Christ into history. A clear delineation of these happenings, he contends, would disclose this creative event and thus enable us to distinguish what was actually the work of God in history from that which merely purports to be of God.

The question that perplexes one who undertakes to relate this analysis of value to the human problem is, How does one pass from the internal anxiety of spirit, which is the existential concern, to this confident, objective pursuit of value, or *vice versa*? The answer can only be that where there is such internal anxiety, confidence in the constructive possibility of criteria or of any instrumental effort to meet man's basic spiritual problem has been impaired, if not altogether dispelled. And, conversely, where such confidence persists, the plight of modern man bordering upon despair, has not actually been faced.

Pragmatism, in its sunnier moods, could well afford to ignore this state of the human psyche because the subjective despair that had driven William James to contemplate suicide had been fully sublimated in the triumph of a philosophical method. This triumph of method meant, in part, an adjustment of the mind to consent to the equating of immediate experience with all of reality. In this swift turn of the mind, the pragmatist was able to dissolve all mystery and all unpredictable elements from experience by taking the known and the knowable datum to be the index of all meaning. Thus the cosmic stretches of time and space could be shrunken to the definable bounds of the social experience. Within this manageable realm, one undertook to carry on a common-sense discourse about man and his problems.

Now there are degrees of abandon with which one will appropriate this method. One can take it simply as a convenience of thought, recognizing the rash, limiting consequences of its oversimplification; in which case, empiricism will always be an approximation toward intelligibility with a clear sense of the unfathomed depths of existence. Or one can employ this method with greater singularity and expectation, counting the practical ends which it can clarify of greater import than the brooding inquiry that rises above this ready-for-action methodology, insistently asking, Can man really know or understand his destiny?

Unconcerned about this brooding inquiry, one can become wholly preoccupied in an instrumentalism, concerned only to wrest from the maze of mystery this tangible structure of meaning that will serve the human good. In time, intimations of distant stars will be more and more obscured by the whirr of engines and by their perpetual cloud of smoke enveloping the city. The mode of inquiry stemming from Francis Bacon, whatever its variation, shunts off pressing human problems of an ultimate character and takes refuge in absorption in more definable tasks.

Now it is possible for a generation or two to be won over to this preoccupation; but when that period is spent and the mind is aroused once again to ponder the brooding inquiry, then the hold of the pragmatic sublimation is dispelled. Modern men are again where William James was when despair gripped his mind.

A method is like a bridge in one respect: it serves to pass over the depth of the ravine so long as there is a supporting terrain at either end. The falling away of such support leaves the bridge suspended or possibly in a condition of collapse. In either case it does not offer passage. It has come to me with increasing conviction that the singularity of method implied in Wieman's pursuit of a criterion of value presupposes a supporting terrain for the pragmatic method. Something, at least, of the pragmatist's procedure persists in his thinking, enabling him, not only to shunt off concern with "domes and spires" that evidence the reach of man's imaginative grasp, but to remain relatively indifferent to problems that are raised by the adumbrative character of experience. He has been one of the first to call our attention to these adumbrations; yet content to remain unaffected by what this observation implies. Clearly it awakens us to problems of faith as well as of value.

Religious naturalism in general, one would have to acknowledge, has been less subtle and sensitive in dealing with the human problem in this respect than have various expressions of supernaturalism. It has been relatively unaware of the literature of despair to which we have just referred. Certainly it has been unresponsive to it except in a few instances. One reason for this is that its problem has never really been an existential one. The problem of faith has not haunted Wieman as it has haunted Barth or Brunner or Niebuhr; or, for that matter, Eliot, Robinson, and Millay. Instead, he has pursued the problem of value with singularity.

This apathy to the problem of faith has led to a two-way insensitivity in Wieman's thinking. On the one hand it has left him virtually indifferent to the anguish of the disillusioned mind; and on the other hand, almost blindly confident in the formulation of a concept of value for solving man's problem, leaving uncalculated the wide disparity between the will to believe and the capacity to believe or to act. One can say that religious naturalism is deficient in its understanding of the affective processes, and of the relation of the affections to the religious enterprise. In this respect it reveals its unreconstructed inheritance from theological liberalism. If it has become realistic about man's illusions and human failings, it has remained relatively naïve in its understanding of man's aspirational life which is the source of his hopes and ultimately of his valuations; and when inverted, the source of his desperate fears, his despair, and his annihilations.

This limitation, I think, prevents a philosophy of religion like Wieman's from informing the human situation in a constructive and persuasive way. He is able to delineate the objective pattern of good as a structure of value, consistent with a given metaphysical view, which the intellect can affirm, appreciate, and cognitively apply in various ways; but the objective so discerned remains as remote and inoperative as the ideals of Absolute Idealism. It is not that Mr. Wieman's philosophy is impracticable in its conceptions; it is simply that his theology does not quicken and impel the whole man. The whole man is man emotionally and imaginatively involved in a cultural tradition with a complex of fears and aspirations, likes and dislikes, capacities and disabilities subtly affecting his conscious and unconscious experience. The emotional rootage of man is a creative source of his action as well as a possible blockage to enlightened behavior. Wieman, in fighting against this possible blockage, attempting to set man's religious life securely upon a verified basis of fact, has, in my judgment, overdone his crusade against religious sentiment and therein has dissociated the vision of the good as an intellectually clarified concept from the vital source of man's motivations, his affections and aspirations. An intellectual asceticism that leaves the springs of sentiment uncalculated becomes naïve in its expectation of response to an intellectual criterion, and undiscerning in respect to sensibilities that inform and restrain the intellect. All philosophical systems tend to err in this direction. The resistance to philosophy in religion and theology may be understood, in part, as a defence against this excess of intellection in the interest of a more total response in man, sometimes designated faith.

We confront a dilemma here which may not be easily resolved. The effort to establish religion upon a verifiable basis invariably leads to an easy capitulation to criteria which, while it may achieve a certain minimal intellectual security, does so at the expense of discounting the emotional depths of man in which issues beyond human comprehension continually disturb the mind. Religion clarified, religion made intellectually secure and valid may find itself emptied of formative power.

On the other hand, indifference to what the intellectual test of truth seeks to establish tends to issue in an easy capitulation to faith which, in many instances, is little more than a desperate emotion or a lapse into sentimental ambiguity. The resolution of this dilemma requires some tempering, both of the concern for intellectual certainty and of the despair that impels the leap of faith. Both are excessive and undiscerning in their own restrictive way.

Certainly religious inquiry must be prepared to acknowledge the vast insecurity that necessarily attends its venture. So much that is significant and relevant is simply beyond human comprehension. And our orientation is not improved by shutting out these disturbing vistas, content to act as if the problem were as simple as we have simplified it to be. The security that we achieve may be necessarily small in proportion to the insecurity that must persist. Whatever balance we achieve between what we know and what we cannot possibly know will offer a partial resolution of this dilemma.

Likewise, the urgency of our predicament, however desperate, can never justify capitulation to despair such that recourse to human discernment, in whatever form, is rejected, Kierkegaard and

Barth notwithstanding. The frail structures of human consciousness, limited and perverted though they may be, nevertheless constitute the instruments of response or interaction through which the divine human encounter has actuality. The effort to counter the arrogance of rationalism invariably leads to an excessive depreciation of the human instrument, just as the effort to correct man's illusions of goodness tends to derogate man to an unbelievably low estate.

When Robinson Jeffers was confronted with an objection to his depreciation of human consciousness in the poem, *Margrave,* where he speaks of the outer stars

> fleeing the contagion
> of consciousness that infects
> the corners of space.[43]

he replied simply that his words exaggerated. "I was irritated into extravagance," he went on to explain, "by the excessive value that people seem to attribute to human consciousness." [44]

Theology is, in part, a poetic enterprise. And the theologian, like the poet, is inclined to resort to

---

[43] "Margrave," in *The Selected Poetry of Robinson Jeffers.* New York, Random House, 1937, p. 366.

[44] Letter, March 1932, quoted by F. I. Carpenter in "The Value of Robinson Jeffers," *American Literature.* Vol. 11, p. 356.

poetic license when the demand for excessive characterization is upon him, often without acknowledging his exaggeration. All theology, in its intensive moods, commits the fallacy of emphasis. In its conscientious concern to destroy the enemy, it may destroy its own sanity, preferring the singularity and decisiveness of the paranoiac to the tempered achievements of the discerning mind.

The problem of achieving greater sensibility in discerning the dimension of thought and feeling which extends beyond clear observation, without abandoning intellectual rigor in the pursuit of observable meanings, is the very problem to which inquiry in the new metaphysics is addressed. Whitehead, for example, who has seen the issue most clearly, presents it, under one aspect, as the problem of prehension; [45] which is not unrelated to the *Gestalt* theory of *isomorphism* or *sensory dynamics* as developed by Köhler.[46] Whitehead sometimes speaks of it as the double significance of the subjective form and the apprehension of an object. Subject-object are not two sharply differentiated entities that may be conveniently or arbitrarily treated as separable; but stand in a context which is, itself, integrating. In any act of perception, the liv-

45 Whitehead, *Adventures of Ideas*, pp. 296ff. See also Dorothy Emmet, *The Nature of Metaphysical Thinking*. London, Macmillan, 1945, pp. 228ff.
46 *The Place of Value in a World of Facts*. New York, Liveright, 1938, pp. 132ff.

ing emotion which attends the apprehension of any object is a relevant part of the datum in understanding the object itself. It cannot be "abstracted from the bare intellectual perception." On the other hand, the bare intellectual perception, which is implied in the conscious discrimination of all descriptive analysis—in psychology as well as in physics, in philosophy and philosophy of religion that pursues a positivistic course—cannot be sustained as adequate description. For "all perception," as Whitehead has said, "is clothed with emotion." [47]

Wherever contemporary thought has been moved by the insight that a relation is a primary datum, it has been compelled to acknowledge a greater complexity than either science or philosophy, in its purely rational forms, has discerned—not only in perception, but in the concrete event itself. No simple intellectualism will satisfy the inquiring mind in these instances. No device, presuming to reduce the data to observable events, will fool the mind into thinking that a simple description of events will yield adequate knowledge. In this, there is a proper reach beyond every form of truncation, whether it is the truncation of philosophical idealism that reduces reality to rationality; or the truncation of radical empiricism that accepts an account of immediate experience as definitive of the

[47] *Adventures of Ideas*, p. 299.

whole of reality; or the truncation of logical positivism that avowedly restricts the realm of meaning to data that can be intelligibly designated by its singularly definitive method.

The rise of this new complex of insight, of which the new metaphysical mood is one expression, is as phenomenal in its way as the reaction of disillusionment and despair, evident in the various forms of existentialism; for it reveals how mountains rise out of ebbing tides. Or, if that figure is obscure, how massive uplifts of constructive thought can accompany the dissolution of hope.

The task of focusing this intellectual revolution for our time into a perspective that will re-illumine the Christian faith remains to be done. This task is not unlike that accomplished by Augustine and Thomas Aquinas, or by Luther and Calvin, when, in their separate ways, they captured the creative currents of thought in their time for a fresh illumination of the Christian faith. This constructive task should challenge our best thinking for the immediate years ahead.

One will see from this analysis that the current theological situation has many facets. One who views it simply as a head-on collision between neo-orthodoxy and liberalism is overlooking one of the real intellectual dramas of history. He is missing an earthquake in his preoccupation with a squall of wind. The import of this new constructive mood that is upon us is, I believe, as significant as that.

The position that I am taking in these lectures, then, is that however much we may disagree with the claims of reactionary or neo-orthodox thinkers, however much we may cling to the concerns of liberalism or to a preference for modern science, we simply cannot grasp the meaning of ourselves or of the human problem except as we take seriously the perspective of man which extends our thinking beyond the observable range of our social experience. In this conviction, stimulated by insights of the new metaphysics, we are led to a rediscovery of the relevance of the Christian faith.

But a simple return to Christianity may avail us very little if all we do is to mouth the phrases that the orthodox creeds have given us. Neo-orthodoxy can become a form of Christian hypnosis or a sedative by which we soothe our perplexed minds into thinking that because we have once again accustomed ourselves to the familiar words of the faith we have recovered the faith. Language and reality are not always the same thing.

Our problem as moderns is to become truly awakened to the meaning of the Christian faith such that it informs and directs and stimulates our corporate and private lives with the same pervasiveness and persistence that the scientific outlook, operating through industry and our business economy, has shaped modern mores. Nothing short of this deep—shall we say—visceral, reorientation of the cultural *elan* in our culture, arising from a re-envisagement of ourselves as creatures of the living God, will really recover for us stature and meaning in living.

The way by which this recovery of Christian faith as a cultural directive in life can be achieved in our time, I hope to make clear in the lecture that follows. I turn now, in concluding these remarks to say a summary word that may focus more sharply the nature of the human problem which is, as we have said, what moves us to a reawakening of Christian faith.

V

What, in brief, is the human problem? The human problem, in its deepest aspect, is not that of survival, or success, or wellbeing, significant as these are in their place. The human problem is meaningfulness in existence, given the fact that both life and death are our lot.

If one must die, what meaning is there in this human existence for any of us? If we are to live, how can we live zestfully toward this inevitable end, that is everyman's portion, with a full sense of stature and significance and creatural fulfilment?

Five years ago this month, I sat in my living room in Claremont, California, with a group of Pomona students. Theoretically we were engaged in a course in America's Spiritual Culture. But war had been declared, and three of the men in the class were leaving for camp at the close of the term. The problem of human culture became peculiarly and poignantly focused in the lives of these three men. There was no false sentiment nor morbidness in the discussion that followed, but our talk turned directly to the problem of death; because these men were confronting the outer limits of life in stark form.

One of the men turned the discussion in this direction, saying, "I find it quite unrealistic to talk about the problem of our spiritual culture when the thing that bothers me most right now is that I may die—before the end of the year perhaps. I don't want to die. I want to live. I have a lot to live for."

The intensity of this moment was broken by a shrill blast of the siren which announced a blackout and the parade of air wardens. Being a block warden myself, I was compelled to don the white helmet and police the block. The three boys, contrary to regulations, made my round with me. (I make this confession now to whatever authorities may be reading these pages.) But the curfew lifted within

less than a half hour, and we returned to our fire-
place to talk far into the night on why men must
die when they want to live.

The boy who asked the question did die. He was
killed two years later while leading an attack on one
of the islands in the Pacific.

Before he fell, he resolved the question for himself in a letter that he had written to his father
which began with the prescient line, "All things
must end that they may continue to begin."

This boy's question is everyman's question.
Whether we ask it or not, our whole life moves toward it in wonder, if not in despair and frustration.

We speak glibly of the fulfilment of life; but
every life remains ultimately unfulfilled, so far as
this span of years is concerned. Moses, sitting upon
the rock looking over the Jordan, hearing the words
of the Lord, "I have caused thee now to see it with
thine eyes, but thou shalt not go over thither" is a
universal symbol, the parable of the unfulfilled life.
All life is lived toward its consummation. Yet every
life must of necessity, so far as these eyes can see,
remain unfulfilled.

Now this one may not agree to; for some lives
seem quite obviously to reach fulfilment—glorious
fulfilment. The tragedy of young life cut off pre-
maturely by war, ill health, or accident, this, one

will say, is clearly unreconcilable, except on faith; yet even here one can find a resolution, saying, "Time is not life; years are not life." Many a person has ended his years at thirty—Mozart, Shelley, Keats, and there was Jesus. How could years add to the stature of their achievements?

You can also say that eternity is in every moment, and to rise above the transciency of time in the realization of what is infinitely greater than all the creations of time, is to embody in each moment of living, or in some moment of living, the utmost of human fulfilment.

Or you can relinquish the reach toward fulfilment, saying this life-process is what it is, with all its mystery and incongruities, its ruthlessness. Yet the will to live is my portion, as it is the portion of every creature that exists. With reverence for life and in dedication to its perpetual renewal, I give myself in service to living creatures, finding in this attachment to life, this praise of life, the very meaning of my own existence.

These are resolutions of the human problem whose saliency I should not wish to deny. They have, in fact, been stages in my own effort to resolve this human problem.

How much we are ultimately dependent upon the mood of relinquishment for giving resolution to this problem, I confess I do not know. Yet relin-

quishment can be in a minor key, or it can be in a
major key. It can be capitulation to despair, as in
Tschaikowsky's *Pathetique*; or in an affirmation that
follows upon the most searching mood of uncer-
tainty, as in the Franck D-Minor Symphony. It can
also be the sure-footed faith of Beethoven, or of
Bach, that sets the inner turmoil of the restless
spirit at rest in the envisagement of objective pattern that delineates purpose and meaning as a consequent of the human reach for spiritual fulfilment.

The Christian faith is in the nature of a Bach
fugue that moves with vigor and profound assurance to complete the yearnings implicit in its initial
theme. It is a reach of imagination, gathering into
its envisagement of existence, the poles of birth and
death.

One of the major premises of our scientific thinking is that we know nothing of beginnings; and we
know nothing of endings. These are lost in mystery.
For the enterprises of fact, we can hardly set this
premise aside; for the study of fact depends upon
observation. Only it becomes clear, in the face of
human tragedy, in the face of the persistent yearn-
ing to understand ourselves against this menacing
background of man's tragic unfulfilment, that this
blunt dismissal of mystery gives us no adequate
orientation for life or for death.

Mystery is always an ingredient of knowledge,

whether acknowledged or not. And for us who are living creatures, it is an ingredient of life. It is one of the deep-seated illusions in our modern thinking that we live in a world of light; or at least, that with our sure methods of thought and experiment we can dispel all mystery and ultimately be lifted from our human darkness.

This we cannot do because, in the context of our existence, darkness is a constituent of our world of light. But to recognize this is to advance beyond that sheer empiricism that seeks to know only the world of light. Empiricism, to gain depth and full dimension, must be aware of light and shadow in its conception of man's destiny. The light is where a criterion of value can give measure and direction to life, for it attends to the creatural existence that has emerged as a human history. The shadow is the penumbra of mystery that is always the deeper dimension of light. Whoever stares into light, as a moth looks into a night flame, will find the light becoming his darkness. The fringe of shadow that is beyond this empirical realm of light is the border of being that is not yet because emergence has reached a stop in us. The psychical thrust is temporarily arrested in the human life span; but this is not to say that it is fully contained within the empirical meanings which we are able to designate.

Any theology, if it is to articulate the deeper

dimension of empiricism must be attentive to this margin of the life process that seems to give hint of a farther range of human destiny. Except as it brings this more tenuous aspect of the life-process (the aspect where life borders upon death) into genuine continuity with the more evident and observable area of experience to which a criterion of value can rightfully apply, empiricism cannot do justice to the sense of depth in existence, or to the tragic sense, both of which are dimensions of experience that derive from the realization that the span of evident experience rides upon a vast ocean of yet unexplored possibilities of meaning and existence. The island character of life's enterprise is a fact not to be lost sight of in any religious interpretation of experience; for in this imagery of existence the true nature of the life-process is revealed: an upsurge of visible terrain in the midst of vastness which we cannot explain. Positivism did lose sight of this fact. And we, today, may well lose sight of it if concern for observable events leads us so far inland as to lose sight of the water's edge.

We get pattern in existence and a clue to its ultimate meaning when, beyond our preoccupation with social experience, which we can clearly understand, we become sensible to what is beyond comprehension, seeing our existence as more than the interim life-process since it is inclusive of the mys-

teries of both birth and death. It is this dimension
of the human problem that is provided by the
Christian faith. And it is this dimension which must
be restored to our thinking upon man before the
nature of the human problem can be adequately envisaged.

CHAPTER TWO

The Meaning of the Christian Faith

THE RESTRICTIVE VIEW OF THE HUMAN LIFE-SPAN, centering upon the interim between birth and death without being attentive to the mysteries that enclose our daily lives, cannot give an adequate understanding of the nature of the human problem. Important as our social and humanistic sciences are, and the educational and religious efforts that are based upon these sources of insight, they cannot be made alternatives to this deeper inquiry and to this larger affirmation which has always concerned the Christian faith.

I

It remains for us now to inquire into the meaning of the Christian faith which we thus advance as an imperative for the modern mind in search of life's meaning and concerned with the resolution of our deepest yearnings.

I have no intention here of recounting the formal declarations of any creed or of defending the claims of any authoritarian view. What I hope to accomplish is that kind of sensitive selection of the elemental meanings implicit in all the many formulations of Christian doctrine which will disclose what is seminal in the Christian faith, and enable it to become living and compelling in our own time and culture.

I must first say a word about the approach to the historic faith which is impressing itself upon theologians today. I do not say that all theologians find it persuasive; but many do. And I count myself among them.

It is an approach that takes the import of the myth seriously. Now immediately I have lost the confidence of some readers because in many circles, the word "myth" is regarded as thoroughly unrespectable and unreliable. Among modern scholars in theology and philosophy, however, and I should add in cultural anthropology as well, this word carries new illumination.[1] Bear with me as I try to make my case with you.

[1] Berdyaev, N., *Spirit and Freedom;* Bevan, E., *Symbolism and Belief.* London, Allen and Unwin, 1938; Cassirer, Ernst, *An Essay on Man.* New Haven, Yale University Press, 1944; Emmet, Dorothy, *The Nature of Metaphysical Thinking.* London, Macmillan, Ltd., 1946; Malinowski, B., *Myth in Primitive Psychology.* New York, Macmillan, 1926; Marett, R. R., *Faith, Hope, and Charity.* New York, Macmillan, 1932; Niebuhr, R., in *The Nature of Religious Experience* by Bewkes, Bixler, Calhoun, et al., New York, Harper, 1937; Niebuhr, R., *Beyond Tragedy.* New York, Scribner's, 1937; Tillich, Paul, *The Religious Situation.* New York, Holt, 1932; Urban, W. M., *Language and Reality.* London, Allen and Unwin, 1939; Whitehead, A. N., *Religion in the Making.* New York, Macmillan,

Anthropologically, myth is, first of all, "a cultural force," to quote Malinowski.[2] It is a statement of primeval reality which still lives in present-day life and offers justification for precedent. "Myth," Malinowski continues, "serves principally to establish a sociological charter, or a retrospective moral pattern of behavior. It fulfils a function closely connected with the nature of tradition, with the continuity of culture, with the relation between age and youth, and with the human attitude toward the past. Myth is an indispensable ingredient of all culture. . . . Myth is a constant byproduct of living faith." [3]

The concept of the myth is freely employed by us in speaking of other religious faiths, for we are able to view their cultures objectively enough to see the tenuous strands of primeval reality that spread like gossamer throughout those cultures. One can see, for example, the myth of Karma and transmigration of the later Vedas giving direction of meaning to all India touched by Hindu faith. One can see the myth of the Bodhissatvas in the Mahayana Buddhism—the Buddhist foregoing the luxury of personal extinction in the interest of others yet un-

1926; *Symbolism*. New York, Macmillan, 1927. Wieman, H. N., *The Source of Human Good*. Chicago, University of Chicago Press, 1946. Langer, Suzanne, *Philosophy in a New Key*.

  [2] *Myth in Primitive Psychology*. New York, Macmillan, 1926.
  [3] *Ibid*.

delivered. One can see the myth of Islam giving pattern to Mohammedan culture, setting it clearly enough apart from Christian and Jewish life, although it rests back upon traditions that are continuous with these two faiths. So in the cultures of Europe and America where the Christian faith has settled like an enveloping climate upon the generations, the persistent effect of its myth has given shape to its traditions and social mores.

This need not mean that the Christian West has acknowledged this influence of the myth, or yielded to its force. In fact, quite the contrary has been increasingly evident. European history has been rife with protest and rebellion against this faith. And American history, almost as a continuous account, is the story of dissociation from its claims. We have lived under an arrangement of separation of Church and State from the time of our inception as a nation which in its way has served to restrain the interchange of Christian and democratic insights. But no student of cultural history is fooled by protests or by disavowals, or even by dissociations. For negations, too, are culturally determined and determining. And negations shape the cultural pattern as profoundly, often, as do affirmations. The net result is different, to be sure; but the fact remains that the Christian myth, as a cultural force, whether approved or rejected, has continued through all these centuries to give a certain character, a certain pattern, to the emotional and cognitive life of Europe and America.

The mistake of Christian scholars often is that they give careful attention to the approving side of this impact, but minimize the other aspect; hence Christian history gets distorted, perhaps only half told. The story of heaven is not complete without an adequate account of the revolt of the angels; thus hell is a major sub-topic in the history of heaven.

If one approaches an understanding of Christian faith from the view of cultural history, one is led to ask, What is the motif of this human venture in its most comprehensive aspect? How would one discover this? Well, where do such motifs generally become manifest? They appear in the most profound areas and in the most simple areas of man's experience. They infect the thinking of the sages, and they rise up in modest form in the exultant or the desperate utterances of common people. A canvassing of metaphysical and devotional writings, or attentiveness to prayers and the pious discourse of people would therefore reveal to one outside our culture something of the bare outlines of this controlling myth.

Were one to pursue the investigation further, one would find the pattern disclosing the motif taking form in the literature, painting, sculpture, song, and cathedral structures of successive ages. Then were he to enter the cathedral or the church building, and observe the people at worship, he would exclaim, "Here it is, more or less complete!" I say more or less, because it is not likely that any one group of Christians at worship would reveal the whole myth. It is not clear what one would note in every case, but certain features would undoubtedly loom above all others: the name, Jesus Christ, the Cross, the name God, Our Father, Almighty King, etc., the words Creator, Redeemer; perhaps the words love, sin, salvation.

The function of the myth is not to give definitive meaning to any reality, experience, or event; but to associate experience with the ultimate reality or event—to keep experience alive and sensitive to what lies beyond the borders of one's being. Myth reaches beyond the social experience, though it is inextricably bound up with the social experience. It is the language of indirection by which the events of the social experience are heightened and chastened by a vision of experience in its ultimate relations.

The myth has always served this function in the ritual drama. One can say that the ritual of the Roman Catholic mass serves this purpose, and could serve it less restrictively were it not given literal force. In Protestantism we have retained certain features of the Christian drama in worship, though there has been a conscious effort here to extend this literalizing force even more. Yet the reading of the *Word*, as in the Lutheran service, remains a dramatic act; and the service of Communion in all of the Protestant churches, continues this language of indirection, saying with symbol and movement and attitude and the felt experience, vastly more than could be communicated with words. And increasingly, Protestant groups have begun to rediscover the Scriptures in their dramatic medium, i.e., in a medium that achieves this indirect reference that is characteristic of all art—a pointing of the human spirit, its hopes and aspirations, beyond itself.

The choir has become for Protestant worship a saving force in this dramatic and mythical sense. Such rapport with the Christian myth as one gets in Protestantism as a continuous experience, comes through the singing of the great epic utterances— the Palestrinas and the chorales of Bach, for example, Brahms' *Requiem*, Handel's *Messiah*, Bach's *Cantatas*. It may also come from the reading of such literature as Dante's *Divine Comedy*, Milton's *Paradise Lost*, Bunyan's *Pilgrim's Progress*, or Thompson's *The Hound of Heaven*. It is achieved through drama that is consequential enough in theme to stretch the mind toward large ideas of human destiny.

Myth continues to operate in our consciousness, in other words, through poetry, song, and drama; and through these mediums the mind is stretched toward the illimitable and given an orientation that brings stature and responsiveness to spirit.

What I am trying to say is that the myth, in any culture, is significant with meaning and living force far beyond the definitive meaning which can be distilled from it. And the Christian myth in our culture, a myth that affirms a deeply rooted insight concerning God's creative activity, man's nature, and the relationship between man and God, has significance for us far beyond the literal meanings that various theologies have distilled from the assertion.

There is a sense in which all theology is but a footnote to these magnificent declarations in poetry, song, and drama. It is the explicative accompaniment. But the theologian is often insensible to the truth of poetry, and his appreciation of the significance of art and drama in the communication of insight is often meager. Thus, his labors offer but a shabby commentation upon these vistas of the inspired word of Scripture as compared, for example, with its heightened rendering in a Bach B-Minor Mass, or a Brahms' Requiem.

The literalist, whether he is a theologian, a religious educator, preacher, or parishioner, has often been religion's real, though unintentional, enemy.

(Or, to be more generous, perhaps we should say, liability.) For the literalist has persistently failed or refused to rise to the elevation of insight to which the seers and prophets and poets of the faith have beckoned their people. The literalist simply will not be reverent before ideas or emotions that transcend his understanding; or stretch his mind to become sensible to them; nor will he pay the price of long vigils, or climb Calvary's peak to prepare for a deeper understanding. His thought moves in a single key—that to which his restricted mind has become accustomed. And except as these high things are brought down to him in rational guise, they are as nothing before his gaze.

Much that has been written into theology, into creedal documents and catechisms, or even more recently into principles of ethics, or criteria for action, etc., has been this reduction of inspired insight to the rational word, with little effort to retain the qualitative meaning that was implied. Thus much that passes as the explication of the inspired word is little more than the literalist's distortion of a vision for which he has had no capacity to apprehend.

But now, all that I have said here, does not relieve me of an obligation which many a literalist intends —namely to give what the philosopher calls "cognitive meaning" to this outreach of faith—meaning that informs the understanding. This may be quite different from reducing faith to reason. It is rather setting the outreach of faith in an intelligible context such that the language of faith, its hopes and aspirations, become continuous with the reasonable discourse of the culture. This is to render the faith intelligible and relevant to the living culture by bringing it into accord with the sensible experiences of the age, out of which the intelligible responses, informing life and conduct, emerge. This is a task that presses upon anyone who is charged with the problem of communicating alien ideas and feelings, or ideas that transcend generations, such that reinterpretation and revivification are constantly demanded. It is peculiarly the task of the theologian, whose task it is to render the faith intelligible, relevant, and persuasive. I should like to turn to that problem briefly, for some understanding of that task will also give meaning to the Christian faith in its modern aspect.

II

By way of approaching that problem, let me first say a word about the content of faith to which the theologian would give interpretation.

By faith, now, I mean something fairly precise in our experience which connects our lives with all life that has been lived in our culture. I am building here on what Whitehead has called *causal efficacy,*[4] which implies that because time flows, experience is continuous, and the meanings that have emerged, in this space-time continuum, persist in some form to give character to every successive, emergent event. The importance of this insight for theology is that it provides an organic conception of thought and experience in which tradition and the contemporary experience are seen to be integral, rather than two separate, sometimes alien, dimensions of life.

Incidentally this relieves modern thinking of a troublesome problem, especially in theology. The problem of the modernist and the traditionalist has always been a stubborn one. The traditionalist, working from the past, onward, has always seemed to carry in his mind a body of ancient ideas and values which he has sought to superimpose upon the present. The modernist, wholly immersed in the present, has seemed to cut himself off from the past in such a way that he could not connect himself or his ideas in any fruitful way with his inheritance. Any effort to bring the traditionalist and the modernist together has resulted in a rather mechanical arrangement in which the past and present were patched together somehow, but never in a way that

[4] *Process and Reality.* New York, Macmillan, 1929.

revealed their interpenetration and creative relationship.

In the view that I am presenting here, faith is understood to be this inheritance of Christian insight and valuation upon experience which persists among us as in a protoplasm, carrying into our generation, the persisting propulsions, sentiments, and hopes that have defined our spiritual outreach through the centuries in which our culture has been emerging. It is not something back there to which we go, but something living in our lives, however dormant, awaiting resurrection and creative connection with our lives.

What is this faith that resides in our cultural experience like a protoplasmic nucleus of seminal insight? Obviously you cannot pick it out and designate it, or describe it so as to make it singularly bared. What is deepest in a personality or a culture cannot be so extricated. Its propulsions, sentiments, and hopes are like the subtle rhythms of the sea that move the tides in and out. Were these propulsions, sentiments, and hopes as assured and uninhibited as the rhythms that carry the tides, this spiritual depth that is in our culture and in each of us would be a mighty movement toward the increase of good in life. But faith in our culture is of meager momentum. Such faith as persists in our institutions, our homes, our schools, even in many of our churches, is like a power that is spent, almost vestigial in its total effect, as if designating a capacity in our natures that is no longer functional.

Yet the conditioning that issues from these deeps in our nature, however impaired, however blocked or frustrated, shapes our living and our cultural expression, if only in affecting our negations, or suppressed impulsions, or the peculiar way in which we dissipate our creative powers. It determines, too, the course of the perversions of our spiritual heritage. Where, for example, could you find egoism and individualism running rampant except in a culture where the sacredness of life in the individual had emerged as a spiritual sentiment? Where could you find this exaggerated zeal for standard of living, for the abundance of life's goods, except in a cultural history that has affirmed life? World and life-denying cultures, as in certain oriental peoples, are not easily won to misplaced enthusiasms in this form. Where could you find such readiness to ignore the sins of the present, to postpone the decisive issues of life, except in a religious culture where forgiveness has been made an ingredient of faith, and expectancy gives promise of a future? That history will save us, is a conviction that can sanction indecisiveness, as it has done in certain periods of our national life.

Without exercising the positive values of faith, a people can express its conditioning through its perversions of the spirit. In many ways, we give evidence of being a Christian culture in reverse, of being a social inversion of the faith that we possess.

A faith, when it cannot be pervasive in a culture, may gather into hardened and congealed areas that become insulated from the living culture. Here faith becomes formalized and transformed into an esoteric stimulus that tends to alienate its people from the demands of the culture. In this form, religion uproots life. Faith, then, no longer functions as a spontaneous and deep propulsion to live in community and to serve the creation of good; but in this formalized state, it tends to atrophy the will to live creatively within culture. Thus the exercise of faith in such segregated ways, where the church becomes an insulated tradition instead of a resource of qualitative meaning and stimulus for the community, can be another expression of the perversion of faith.

This may seem like a hard statement, but it seems to me true that certain outstanding institutions of Christianity in our day have brought the Christian faith into this congealed state.

The formalizing of religious sentiments has gone far in our society. We have only to think of such words as love, sin, grace, redemption, sacrifice, the

cross, life eternal. These are wonderful words! They
are perhaps the strongest words in our vocabulary.
They are words that envisage the farthest reaches
of our destiny. They are universal words. They ad-
dress man as creature. They lift up the concerns of
man, beyond which there is nothing more important
—for they point man to the sovereign source of his
being.

Yet these words have become stereotyped. Our
use of them in religious discourse is repetitious. And
the way we use them restricts their meaning, restricts their sphere of relevance, brands them as
theological words. The moment they are mentioned
in the general culture, in educational groups, in
artist groups, among literary people, you feel the
withdrawal, the impatient silence, as if an alien discourse had intruded. This betrays our condition. It
reveals our problem. We suffer in part from a
formalism of the concepts and insights which carry
the most seminal meanings for our existence.

I haven't a clear notion as to how this condition
can be overcome. It arises, as you see, from an impasse between religion and culture which nullifies
at the outset the impact of religion upon culture,
and leaves culture itself, in its literary as well as in
its economic and political expression, uninformed
and untempered by the discipline of being aware of
an ultimate concern. Freeing religious insight from

its formalisms may come about in two ways: (1) by cultural mediums outside the church becoming carriers of these insights, as when art and literature in their distinctive ways achieve a spiritual intent; (2) or through a renascent church that finds a way of escaping its formalisms.

It has happened that literature and art have, in themselves, re-created these words for civilization. This happened in Dante's time in his writing of the *Divine Comedy*, and in seventeenth-century England when Milton wrote *Paradise Lost*. To a degree, modern poetry and drama have re-created our feeling for these seminal words, not only in verse and drama that is tradition-bent, as in T. S. Eliot's *Murder in the Cathedral* and *The Hollow Men*, or in his essays, *The Sacred Wood*, but in poetry like Stephen Vincent Benet's *John Brown's Body*, and Thornton Wilder's *Our Town*. The creative mind, whenever it deepens its grasp of experience to an elemental perception, may become a powerful aid to the human imagination in recapturing its spiritual force.

Curiously enough, the art of the novel has become fairly effective in chronicling the sins of the human spirit, as in Dreiser, Joyce, and Sinclair Lewis; or in delineating the disintegration of human personality as in Somerset Maugham; but it has yet to grasp the meaning of grace and redemption and to treat them with something more than a sentimental or trivial hand.

The church is in need of the creative artist's subtle and discerning hand, even in its task of renascence; for without such aid, its effort to find release from formalism may not turn out so well. Let me just say at this point that the opposite of formalism is not formlessness; but creativeness. And the effort to put life in religion by spreading informality through every function of the church, may serve no purpose except to exchange austerity and impotence for indulgent sentiment. This is no easy problem, and one in which the churches must have every sympathy. Nevertheless, it remains true that the force of religious communication is seriously impaired because the arts of communication within the churches are unequal to the great meanings for life that it has in its heritage to communicate.

The faith that now appears to lie dormant beneath the formalisms of religion and the cultural accumulations of the years is the formative myth of our culture which recites in dramatic metaphor, the deepest and gravest characterization of man's nature and destiny. It is this tale that provides the human being in our culture with scope and stature and enables him to see the human creature in the large setting of creation and fulfilment.

Can this drama of redemption be stated in an all-inclusive way so that the motif of theological reflection is made clear? Actually, the drama is well known to all of us. It may be stated in ten sentences:

The Drama

1. God created man and woman.
2. Man was good, woman was good.
3. But man and woman sinned, and God's wrath was aroused causing judgment to fall upon human life.
4. Suffering and sorrow filled the earth.
5. And the cry of men was heard by God.
6. God said, I will restore man's fallen self; I will create a new order of man; I will, myself, descend to earth in the form of man and draw fallen man into a new life.
7. So God was in Christ, reconciling the world of men to him; but the world did not receive him; they crucified him.
8. Yet in this broken life, men saw the new light, and the tragedy of the rejected gift of grace was overcome by the resurrected life.
9. The resurrected life is the recreation of man, born of sorrow and man's rejection, the child of suffering, life rising out of a broken life; all men to be whole and renewed must be so broken and resurrected.
10. Thus, is man redeemed from a nature willful and unrepentant; thus is he restored to wholeness which is oneness with God; thus is he healed from his brokenness, the new life is born.

Now the valuations that arise from this elemental myth of our culture can be stated as follows:

1. That life is good, being the structures created

by the Creator for the attainment of spirit in His image.

2. That the individual life is sacred and meaningful in the drama of creation.

3. That an expectancy attends every created individual for the realization of his fulfilment.

4. Yet, that human fulfilment is not linear, not the mere process of self-realization, for man's powers are impaired by the fact of his individuality which sets him at tension, both with his Creator and with the community of all creatures.

5. Thus the sheer clinging to the concerns of one's individual existence, untempered by sacrificial love, retards, rather than advances, one's fulfilment.

Life oriented toward sacrificial love, the readiness to "lose oneself for His sake," is the Christian transmutation of the attachment to life (that is evident in the nature faiths, for example) carrying the assurance that "he who so loseth his life shall find it."

The full meaning of this transmutation of the attachment to life, by which "the wall of individuality is breached," to use Mr. Wieman's phrase, and by which the community of one's life with all men and with God is attained, is the Christian idea of redemption. Life is broken, and thereby renewed and fulfilled.

There are many other strands of meaning that

derive from this elemental myth and which have worked into the fabric of our western experience, but these may serve to point up the motif of our continuing culture which gives it its peculiar character, its inclinations, and its tendency toward a sense of meaning and of value in living. Not that all men in our culture accept and emulate this vision of man, but that even in their disavowal of it, they bear its imprint in the way in which their disavowal or rebellion is expressed.

The great classical systems of Christian thought are constructions of thought and ritual based upon this elemental drama of redemption. They are not just any kind of construction. Theology is like architecture: it has its focal point which gives the center of balance from which all subsequent building proceeds. Any form of art which has design proceeds this way. The focal point of a theology reveals a great deal about the theology itself and about the religious cult or culture that arises from this center. For example:

1. The focal point of Roman Catholic thought has been consistently the sacrifice of Christ, or the death of Christ, symbolized by the Cross. This is the event of climax in the religious drama enacted at the altar in the Mass. This has given a distinct quality or tone to the Roman service of worship,

as Frederich Heiler points out in *The Spirit of Worship*.[5] It has also determined Roman Catholic architecture, with its elevation of the Cross at every point, not only in the altar symbolism, and the symbolism dominating the exterior; but, as in the great medieval cathedrals, the floor-plan of the worshipping structure or church.

2. The focal point of the Eastern Orthodox Church, of which the Russian Orthodox Church is representative, has been, not the Cross as symbol of Christ's death, but the affirmation beyond the Cross, which declares, "He is risen." The faith of the Russian Orthodox Church and of the Greek Orthodox Church may be said to be the continual celebration of the Easter message. It is the Eastern church in a symbolic as well as in a geographical sense. Here again, the joyousness of this faith, bordering upon religious ecstasy, and childlike wonder, has its root in what it has found to be focal in the elementary drama. One can sense this listening to the liturgical music of the Russian church, in contrast to the sobering music of the Latin mass.

3. The focal point of theology and worship in the Lutheran Church is the proclamation of the word *(Das Wort Gottes)* which is the good news of God's grace. This fact was impressed upon my mind with peculiar effectiveness one Sunday morn-

5 New York, Harper, 1927.

ing, sitting in a service of worship in the University Church in Marburg, Germany. It was my first Sunday in Marburg. Citizens of the community and university people had gathered in the age-old church in considerable numbers. The service was ready to begin: the organ was playing, and the people seemed attentive as if awaiting a cue; but the minister had not yet appeared. Suddenly, unannounced and without evident prompting, the entire congregation burst into song. They had no hymnals. They apparently needed none. The liturgy was thoroughly familiar to them. The congregational singing continued for several minutes, with the organist playing interludes between the hymns. Finally the minister appeared at the lectern and led the congregation in responsive reading, following which another hymn was sung. During the singing, the minister mounted the pulpit stairs, the pulpit being to the right of the nave and raised several feet above the congregation. At the conclusion of the hymn, the minister, in ringing tones, announced: *"Hören Sie das Wort Gottes!"* ("Hear the Word of God!") I can still feel the awesomeness of that event. The congregation as one man rose to its feet with an air of expectancy that was unmistakable. I knew then what was meant by the remark that the Lutheran service centers around the proclamation of the Word. The reading of the Word was nothing short of a sacramental act, eliciting a numinous experience in those who participated.

4. The focal point of Calvinistic theology and of Calvinist worship is the *adoration of God,* arising from the centrality of the sovereignty of God. All else is secondary. Any expression of mediation, moderating the stark fact of God's sovereignty, is anathema. Enhancements in worship that seek to soften the austerity of the religious relationship are likewise tabu. God in his moral starkness, unrelieved by asethetic concessions is a prevailing emphasis in the Calvinist faith.

Always some structure of thought has been available in the culture in the form of a controlling concept which has served to give intellectual force to the insights of the faith within the general discourse of society, sufficiently at least, so that these sentiments which can inform men's wills, temper their passions, and inspire their motives, can become genuinely incorporated in the cultural life, both as an acidual cleansing and as a directive of man's common life.

This Christian assurance can be advanced simply as a faith to which men's hearts and minds may respond as it often has been. The notable example is the preaching of Martin Luther. And, in the main, one can say, all Protestantism has inclined toward this presentation of it. One can make a strong case for saying that Protestant theologians have been peculiarly indifferent to philosophy and metaphysics as an aid to the interpretation of the Christian faith. And the neo-orthodox theology of Karl Barth is thoroughly consistent with this tendency.

Ultimately, I should agree on the primacy of faith, for when we come to the frontiers of our being, where light borders on darkness, we must all stand in wonder and in faith; or be engulfed by despair. But what determines our ability to embrace this farther range in wonder and in faith may be the inclination of our being made possible by the meager understanding of our existence as an intellectual problem. This is the force of what we may call the empirical ground of faith. Not that this experience explains our destiny, but that it sets our thought in a perspective that can provide a clue to life.

A faith that can rest only on sentiment fails in its corporate responsibilities as a stimulus and as a clarification of life's processes. It is significant that where Protestantism has rested with full weight upon faith it has failed to develop a social philosophy of life. And this, as Paul Tillich has said, is the source of the real peril of Protestantism.[6]

What determines the focal point of a theology or of a liturgy at any one time is not altogether

---

[6] *The Religious Situation.* New York, Holt, 1932.

clear. Within certain periods of thought, or within a cultural experience, a motif prevails, in part the coloring of the mood, as for example: the pathos and sacrifice of Calvary expressing the Latin mind; the joy of resurrection in the Eastern mind; the anguish over sin, finding resolution in the assurance of Grace through the proclamation of the Word in German Lutheran theology, communicating overtones that cannot readily be given cognitive meaning; and adoration, in its stark simplicity, voicing the objective feeling of Calvinism. One does not look about for a focal point in theology. This comes to the thinker or worshipper out of the resources of thought and feeling that are available to experience in that particular moment of history. It is a point of perspective that presents itself to the mind seeking cognitive illumination of that which reaches the affections through tradition or through the nurture of faith.

Conceptually, this focus is a controlling idea of the culture at large. How it emerges, is a problem in the history of ideas. But all of culture at any given period of time is shaped and, as it were, is held within an ideological orbit by some luminous insight, out of which forms a distinctive pattern of thinking, peculiar to the age, providing for that era its form of intelligibility. Ancient, as well as new and alien ideas are made intelligible by relating them to this luminous center of thought. And by being made coherent with this frame of reference, such ideas are commended to the affections and made emotionally acceptable as well.

A controlling idea of this kind becomes the point of entry through which inherited insights and propulsions of faith are assimilated into the current discourse of a culture. That is, they are made intelligible ideas, relatable to the general context of ideas. Thus, through the dynamics of thought and language, spent ideas and sentiments awaken to a new life-span, as it were.

III

Now I submit that the idea Creation, or Creative Activity, is such a controlling idea in our time. It would take a great deal of elaboration to show how this idea has emerged in our culture at this particular time to assume so formative a role in thought. There is probably not a field of thought or experience in contemporary life in which the peculiar coloring and direction is not given by this idea. In its most recent formulation it finds expression in the word *emergence*.

It is not accidental that the impressive metaphysics of Whitehead should have appeared in the form in which it has at this juncture of history, fusing the ideas of emergence and feeling. Nor is it accidental that psychiatry, with its stress upon empathy, sensibility, and creative experience, should appear at the same time. Likewise with *Gestalt* psychology and the social concept of the self in Mead's philosophy; all of these solutions to problems in various fields of thought express affinity with a *wisdom*, shall we say, a pervasive assumption, a bent of insight, that defines our climate of thought as distinct from every previous period of thought that we can recall.

One can say that the wisdom of our times, rising, no doubt, out of accumulative thought and experience, turns constructive thought, of whatever field, in a certain direction, which direction is given in the elaboration of the controlling idea.

Reactionary thought presents quite a different matter. Reaction is never prompted by a creative impulse; but by a resistance to implications of the existent situation in thought. Reaction seeks a different orientation from the existing one by recovering a perspective that has been relinquished. In this recovery of an earlier orientation of thought, the focal idea that gave formulation to thought and feeling in a previous period of culture is intruded into the contemporary period—always with a certain sensitivity to the problem of making it relevant, though not necessarily in a constructive way. Relevance is achieved necessarily through apologetic effort that translates the ancient concept into a modern meaning.

Neo-Reformation theology and Neo-Thomism seem to me to be prompted by such an impulse, and therefore stand outside of the dynamics of thought which are shaping the structure of meanings in our modern discourse. Neo-Reformation theology bears some affinity with all strands of existentialism which despair of constructive formulations. Significant as these forms of thought are in our day as intellectual and aesthetic formulations of the mood of despair which grips our age, they do not open the way for constructive effort in thought. By their premise of despair, and their conscious isolation from the dynamics of thought they acknowledge a resignation of constructive effort in this direction.

Constructive theology, in so far as it pursues a formulation of the cognitive meanings of the Christian faith in the context of structural meanings that provide intelligibility in our time, has no alternative but to follow the procedure that has given rise to systematic theology in former periods of reconstruction—namely, of setting the sentiments of the Christian myth in the philosophical context that elaborates the controlling idea.

Creation, or creativeness, it may be objected, is not a distinctively Christian concept; it is Hebraic or Greek. Thus to make it the focal point of a Christian theology is to force theology at the outset

out of its Christian orbit. This overlooks the significance of the focal point in any theology. It is its
nature to be in some sense outside of the common
discourse of Christian thought until it has been
made the organizing center of the new Christian
ideology. Sacrifice is such a non-Christian concept
absorbed into Christian thought and feeling. Logos
is another. Rationality, as in Thomism, is yet another. Even the idea of proclamation and the Word,
the idea of adoration, arising from God's sovereignty, are importations in the sense that they were
appropriated at a given time and place under special circumstances as intelligible concepts in a time
when they had become pervasive in the culture,
around which to organize the Christian message.

One can say that the procedure of interpreting
the Christian faith in terms of a controlling concept
in any given age is simply the act of integrating the
imagery of the faith with the intelligible discourse of
the age. It is the way by which the sentiments of
faith take on cognitive force and become relevant
qualifications to human thought and action.

IV

The new orientation of thought, then, which
promises to give intellectual force to the reawakening of the Christian consciousness in our time, cen-

ters about the concept of creation—the emergence
of spirit as a psychical thrust that carries the structures of reality to successive levels of emergence.
This movement of thought is, to my mind, the only
impressive alternative to neo-orthodoxy. Its strength
lies in the fact that it has been pervasive and il-
luminating in almost every field of thought and
really constitutes the controlling concept of our
age.

The most comprehensive statement of this new
metaphysics has been given by Alfred North
Whitehead in *Process and Reality,* an exceedingly
difficult book, even for the skilled reader in metaphysics. A more readable statement of his view is
in his *Adventure of Ideas,* which Whitehead, himself, regarded as his best book. When *Process and
Reality* was first published in 1929, one reviewer
wrote, "Not many people of our generation will
read this book, for it is difficult reading; yet I venture to say that it is the most important book in the
field of thought since Aristotle's metaphysics." I
should like to add that the metaphysics of Whitehead could prove as formative for Christian thought
in our time as Aristotle's metaphysics was during
the rise of Thomism in the thirteenth century, and
as neo-Platonism had been in shaping Augustine's
theology.

I am centering here upon what seems to me to be

the crucial insight in Whitehead's metaphysics and which is a key insight for giving fresh illumination to the force of Christian faith. This insight is the creative act of God, or more particularly, that happening in creation by which feeling is infused into brute process, giving actuality to tenderness, meaning, and beauty. This, I would make the focal point of the new theology that is emerging.

Whitehead's metaphysics, like other efforts in this field, is the attempt to state in comprehensive terms, the processes and their qualifying influences, which occur in every event of creation. The gist of this analysis is that every event of creative happening, whether it is the birth of a child, the emergence of friendship, or the growth of a village, is a happening in which sheer force or process is chastened, sensitized, directed toward more tender meanings than its bare, brute form would intend. The creative act, wherever it occurs, is process yielding to a tender working, such that the power implicit in the process becomes creative and sustaining of the value that thus emerges. The burst of bloom on the desert, as the squatty yucca plants send up their whitened flares, gives a clear feeling of this grace in nature, softening and tenderizing what would otherwise be shorn of grace and meaning. This is creation in the desert sand, carrying the brute force in the midst of the wasteland to visual fulfilment.

And the earth was without form a void; and darkness was upon the face of the deep. And the spirit of God moved upon the face of the waters.

When it was morning, God took the good earth and held it to his lips, and breathed upon it, breathed silently upon the dry earth.

Each event of human birth is a repetition of this age-old happening within the maternal womb. Creativity attended by a gentle working, intent on higher meaning, creates the child as the pregnant mother yields her body up to this miracle. When a child grows, creation anew is occurring within a single life-span. The waters of the deep are opening up again. A firmament is taking form. The patient hand of the Creator is intruding upon a chaotic flood to give gentle direction to this emerging event.

This tender working becomes evident in the forming of skills. We say it becomes evident, though we mean it can be discerned over a period of time. It is not immediately observed. It gradually intrudes upon our consciousness as we become aware of emerging qualities of behavior in ourselves or in others, in contrast to performances previously recalled. Though our envisagement of this process is now imaginative, recalling this working of events, the forming of skills is not imagined; it has happened as a series of unobtrusive events which now present effects, real effects, which can be observed and appreciated.

The forming of skills is not the person's doing; this is what has happened to him in response to what he or she has done in the way of attentive acts. But this forming of the skill is like the emerging of order; in fact is precisely the emerging of a particular order of responses which now has become dependable, even automatic, by reason of the growth of connections which has followed upon the person's attentive acts. The miracle of life is nowhere more evident than here, which is why schools and the age of youth will forever occupy a foremost place in human interest.

This miracle occurs in the writing of a poem. Creating a poem is, in this sense, not the poet's doing alone, but a pressure of sensitivity that happens to him under the stimulus of some acute emotion or some rare perception that shapes the responsive and sensitive consciousness toward this unique expression. When the poem takes form, what appears may seem to the poet, himself, something given to him. His powers have produced it, but his powers brought to a peculiar focus and heightened with feeling. So it is in the creation of a symphony, or in the creation of art, or of a life-long companionship, or of a human being, formed by the exigencies of living. These are as beneficent happenings which emerge as something added to effort, very much as a riot of color will come to a woods in autumn, or to a desert in spring: a culmination of many efforts, to be sure; but as a benediction upon it, rather than as sheer result.

In a thousand places over the earth, moment by moment, something of this tenderness and sensitive working appears, subtly and silently turning effort into bloom, or bringing relationships to their ripened issue. It is a process that works on hiddenly until the bloom appears, and by this appearance, events that have long lain hidden, rise into view as we imagine the total working here envisioned.

That tenderness is sovereign over force in every expression of creativity, I submit is the most tremendous idea of history. The insight that this gives the clue to history and to the nature of existence, Whitehead ascribes to Plato. But it was given to the Christian era, he adds, to demonstrate, in fact and in living events, the actual truth of this insight.

The essence of Christianity (he writes, in *Adventures of Ideas*), is the appeal to the life of Christ as a revelation of the nature of God and of his agency in the world. The record is fragmentary, inconsistent, and uncertain. . . . But there can be no doubt as to what elements in the record have evoked a response from all that is best in human nature. The Mother, the Child, and the bare manger: the lowly man, homeless and self-forgetful, with his message of peace, love, and sympathy:

the suffering, the agony, the tender words as life ebbed, the final despair: and the whole with the authority of supreme victory.

I need not elaborate. Can there be any doubt that the power of Christianity lies in its revelation in act, of that which Plato divined in theory? [7]

Then he adds a few pages later:

It is the business of philosophical theology to provide rational understanding of the rise of civilization, and of the tendernesses of mere life itself, in a world which superficially is founded upon the clashings of senseless compulsion.[8]

That tenderness and concern for sensitive meaning are sovereign in life, is the source of the assurance of grace—and of the certainty of judgment. Of this I shall have more to say, for it is the clue to understanding our existence. Our lives, and the life of the world, is the dramatic interplay of force and sensitivity. Brute process like the menacing force that broods over the untamed desert, presses in the nature of man, as in the earth, toward an ultimate dissolution of meaning. Redemption is the continual effort to reclaim force and process within ourselves and within our institutions, for this higher destiny to which the tender working of God points all creation.

[7] From A. N. Whitehead, *Adventures of Ideas.* Copyright, 1933 by The Macmillan Company and used with their permission.
[8] *Ibid.,* p. 218.

The meaning of the Christian faith is in this venture of hope and determination that what has been begun in creation, the turning of sheer process in a sensitive direction, in the emergence of a child or a tender shoot, or in the fruition of the human spirit, shall be carried to an ultimate destiny.

CHAPTER THREE

Understanding Our Existence

THE CHRISTIAN FAITH BEARS WITNESS TO A TEN-
derness in life which moves with restraining influence amid the power-ridden forces of the world,
creating out of its "clashing compulsions" the sense
of meaning, beauty, and goodness. The Christ child
in the arms of the Mother is a touching symbol of
the faith communicating this affirmation. The
Christ on the Cross, and even the Pietàs, revealing
the suffering Christ descended, is this same sentiment set in the context of great anguish. Not only
is this tenderness felt in the pain of the dying figure
and in the remorse and repentance that is elicited by
the realization that this life was broken against the
immovable insensibilities of men, but in the note of
forgiveness as well which rises like the music of an
ensemble of strings to transcend the deeper tones of
anguish and tragedy. Through chorale and altar
flame this witness has been both sung and silently
affirmed.

Is this an illusion of the sentimental mind? Or is
it a true sentiment of our existence, so fundamental,

that apart from it, existence cannot be understood? Tenderness, compassion, concern for beauty, the discriminate and disciplined mind, the affection and praise of companionship, the sentiment of justice and ethical rightness, are these constituents of the life-process, or are they optional in our human enterprise?

The thesis for which we have been contending is that sensitivity in our natures, out of which these graces of the human spirit arise, is the indispensable condition for existence. Without it, actuality could not be. So long as things and people exist, a modicum of sensitivity will be evident; for the very meaning of existence is that brute force has been restrained and turned into meaningful events.

The figure which we advanced earlier in depicting the creative process wherever it occurs suggests a sensitive hand, pressing upon brute process, shaping it into meaningful events, i.e., into events that bear a sensibility to all other events and to the sensitivity of God, himself. This is mythical language, to be sure, by which metaphysics seeks to give application to the insight that feeling, in the sense of empathy, a feeling into other situations to which I am related, is a pre-condition of existence itself.

An example of a human situation which borders upon non-existence, so far as the social reality is concerned, is the schizophrenic personality. Here life is withdrawn into a citadel of its own making. Empathy, the ability to feel, is lacking, hence the condition for creative interaction with the meanings and actual values of the culture is destroyed. Life is at an impasse in these people.

What has become an accomplished fact in the schizophrenic (by reason of accumulative influences, or an initial organic defect in the sensory organism), operates as a potential world phenomenon in institutions, industries, and people in communities, thereby arresting the creative working, or blocking it with their peculiar form of introversion. Here force is made its own sovereign, and the absence of empathy renders whatever power it possesses a threat to all who encounter its influence.

Wherever force is its own sovereign, and the appeal of tenderness is defied or ignored, such that power for its own sake rises to dictate men's course or to lure them into devotion to the pursuit of power, the intent of creation is denied; and the working of God, by which creativeness is carried forward in human structures of consciousness, is defied.

God's work in history is this everlasting operation of persuasion toward meaning, beauty, and goodness. Where this working is sustained, God is upheld in human existence.

The formulation of this fact in Christian theology has generally been stated as the elevation of God's will above the will of man. Augustine, you will recall, puts it this way,[1] as does Calvin;[2] and, more recently, Reinhold Niebuhr in his *Nature and Destiny of Man*. I am suggesting that the fact is somewhat illumined if it is viewed in the perspective of Whitehead's metaphysics, wherein the will of God becomes a creative infusion of feeling or sensitivity by which force becomes meaningful and productive of these tendernesses of life. All existence, all of our existence, may be viewed as the dramatic interplay of force and sensitivity.

As a general observation, then, we can say that any event in society, any social institution, any individual, in which force prevails in disregard of sensitivity, fails of its spiritual intent. Such a person or institution or society becomes a threat to all existence. And conversely, to the degree that a society, a social institution, or an individual embraces sensitivity in its nature as a directive of the force it possesses, it sustains its spiritual intent and becomes a carrier of creativity. This becomes the criterion upon which we judge and understand our existence, a criterion which we derive from an analysis of the creative act itself and which is basic to all existence.

[1] *Confessions.*
[2] *Institutes of the Christian Religion.*

One shrinks from making an appraisal of our public life today on such a basis; for the picture is disheartening indeed, almost beyond hope of recovery. Power, untempered by any of these graces of the spirit, is at a great premium in our day. It is evident in the dominance of the great powers over the lesser powers in world relations. It is evident in the dominance of big business over small business; in the prestige of big educational institutions as compared with smaller schools; in the dominance of large, city churches and their leaders over the more obscure and smaller churches. And within all these institutions, the capitulation to the appeal of sheer power appears in the struggle for power, with little or no concern for the graces that make life kindly, reassuring, beneficent, beautiful, and discriminating.

No aspect of our culture escapes this emulation of power; for it is almost a presupposition of our life that possession of power to coerce or control is indispensable to effectiveness. Thus our political life becomes an assemblage of pressure groups; relations between labor and industrial management become a battle for power; civic life becomes organized pressure of opinion; even religion becomes coercive, in its emulation of other social agencies, and seeks to attain power through numbers and a concerted voice.

I have no concern here to indulge in invectives over the state of our cultural life, though I am convinced, as convinced as I have been of anything in my life, that our society is hell-bent in this accumulative devotion to mass and brute power. One does not need to recall Nazi tyranny, or look across the ocean to Russia; the virus is in our own national life. It has been in our national life since industry began to pyramid its power, and science, supported by technological demands, began to crowd out the concerns of the sensitive life.

The young people on our campuses who say with a certain tone of cynicism, "Keep your uniform in mothballs, soldier; you'll be needing it again!" voice with poignancy the insecurity of our life so long as this power-drive sustains itself.

The one hopeful intrusion upon this complacent drift toward destruction is the concern over the atomic bomb. "The good news of damnation," as Chancellor Hutchins has termed it, thrusts an arresting dart into our thinking. Perhaps this is more pervasive than we are able to imagine. Perhaps, even now, it marks a subtle turning away from our irresponsible era of power-consciousness. There is slight evidence of this in the sober talk among some statesmen and other public leaders. The most arresting evidence is in the aroused conscience of scientists, themselves, who, after all, hold one important key to the new age of power. Their aroused sense of responsibility to the plight of humankind makes a difference which cannot easily be estimated. For their dissociation of science from technology and political ends, except as these are made beneficent enterprises, could create the circumstance for the control and direction of power that is without precedent in our age. A sort of union among scientists in the name of humanity, might extricate scientists from the kind of robot relation to industry which has so greatly accelerated an unsocialized industrial power, and has brought science, itself, to a point where it realizes its own threat to mankind.

The prospects for such re-creation of hope and reassurance are still too tenuous to be counted upon; but whatever looks in the direction of controlling, directing, and sensitizing the vast resources of power that are emerging on the horizon, will be in the right direction. This is the special field of no one; for it is the responsibility of everyone who cherishes existence, itself.

The disregard of the sensitive life, which we must see as our hope in this power age, is supported by a state of mind that is more subtle, and almost more pervasive in its effects, than the blatant adulation of power. That state of mind is to be found quite generally in communities; but it can be detected quite readily in colleges and universities and among the churches. These concentric circles of insensitivity serve to amplify the effect of the pivotal concern with power.

To put it bluntly, our churches and schools as well as our community are not very much concerned with the spiritual life. Oh, we talk a great deal about it. Understood as the creative direction of power through a sensitive concern, the spiritual life suffers greatly in our culture because many, many people dare not acknowledge in their own daily lives, through their own acts of approval or rejection, that a sensitive nature is to be preferred to the insensitive one. They make no issue of it, they simply let their acknowledged preferences settle at a level that is sure to elicit general approval. Their unacknowledged preferences might reveal them to be more discriminating, more responsive to ethical demands, or to the appeal of beauty, or to sentiments of kindness; yet the fear of sentiment and concern lest they should be regarded as soft or sentimental, impel them to shield themselves against this more sensitized side in their natures.

This disregard of the sensitive life may break out with devastating results in a college or university community, especially among students, where a peculiar pose of toughness, with indifference to these goods of life, conceals itself behind a mass-mind of mediocrity. Being a normal person, which, of course, is the desirable person, may thus mean being commonplace in one's intellectual interests and aesthetic appreciations, as well as in one's moral and spiritual sensibilities. Through this blasé public mind, college life can provide a breeding place for this readiness to crush these things of the spirit under a mass rush toward mediocre ends of wellbeing or sheer ambition for status, which is so evident in our public life at large.

A college or university faculty can quickly emulate this trend. So subtle is this influence, that not one of us who works in a college or in a university, can feel delivered from it. The intellectualist, as well as the anti-intellectualist, is capable of succumbing to its lure—the one by assuming a critically, intellectual pose that parades disdain for the things of sensitive feeling, or resists any concession to the appeal of sentiment; the other by relinquishing all responsibility for intellectual and spiritual stimulus, finding rapport with this prevailing, public mind that makes a gospel of the words, "Take it easy!"

So it is within any community. They who dissipate the force of the spiritual life in society are not, in every instance, the ruthless or unadjusted doers of evil; but often the well-adjusted, respected citizens, who nullify, by their indifference to the appeal of excellence, the demands for critical judgment, for taste, for sensibility, for true consideration of the good in society. Even in well-doing, they may degrade the public life.

Assertiveness and the power to impress, may thus become of greater premium than the capacity to be creative, or to serve the common life. The greatest need of our time is to be delivered from this adolescent, super-man complex that persists in adult life, suppressing, or even routing the emergence of mature, spiritual, human beings, for whom the graces and sensibilities of the human spirit are of the very essence of living.

The full import of religion and the moral life, of the philosophic quest, of poetic perception, of appreciative awareness, of the imaginative life in all its forms of expression, will not be persuasive or redeeming in our culture until this maturing of the human spirit advances. And the mounting peril and ruthlessness of our power-driven civilization will, as a matter of course, accelerate, except as this tempering, ordering, sensitizing capacity in ourselves becomes so pervasive that it drastically alters the mores of our modern life.

The mores, in the last analysis, constitute the controls of any society. They provide the gateway through which the grace of God, the sensitive working of His creative hand, can be mediated to human culture; or they provide the barrier to his sensitive working. This is so, because God's working in any age of history, is through the structures of human consciousness which are the actualizing media of his creative spirit.

In lifting up this capacity for sensitivity and tenderness in human nature as the redeeming force in society and in men's lives, I am following through the implication of the thesis which we advanced earlier in making the creative act of God the focal point of the Christian faith.

The whole drama of sin and redemption roots in this creative act. In it, the intention of God is made manifest, namely, to bring into actuality, vivid events of spirit, capable of bearing in their structures of consciousness, the very creativeness that has brought them into being. In this sense, the Creator gives of His sensitive nature to His creatures in the expectation that in them, His spirit will be actualized and enjoyed.

The whole of this mystery we cannot know; but that a sensitivity works in the depths of all of us, and in the world, to realize the fulfilment of spirit, is so evident to the reflective mind that one wonders that it can be so widely missed.

Yet the human situation in each individual life makes the concrete event more obscure and obstructed than may appear to the reflective mind. For in each of us the storms of creation itself rage.

We are not placid pools upon which the tender and beneficent intentions of God fall as a mist; we are floods and turbulent streams in which brute process presses ruthlessly on without intent, restrained only by the balance of tenderness, sensibility, and empathy which holds us in existence as actualized events. No imagery adequately seizes the full meaning of this fact. Historic theologies have likened our natures to the confluence of the powers of good and evil, light and darkness, spirit and flesh, the image of God and the willful spirit of man. Our recent psychological literature portrays us as potentially divided selves, responding to evident, conscious stimulus, on the one hand, and to repressed, subconscious drives on the other. These all have their illumination. They are all mythical devices, as imaginative media must be, for wresting some clue to fathom the mystery of our existence. But the one clear feeling that we get from all of these unsatisfactory devices is the complexity of human nature that impels it both to respond to and to resist the appeal of its spiritual intent.

This, in brief, is what the Christian faith has traditionally meant by the drama of sin and redemption, insisting that obstructions existed in human nature which precluded the completion of the creative act of God in man. And no simple removal of these obstructions, such as man himself might devise, would rid human nature of that which defies the creative spirit. For this is inextricably involved in existence, itself, as process is related to purpose; or force to sensitivity.

That this creative working is blocked in us, even as it is partially fulfilled, is to be explained by the predicament of our existence, which requires us to be individuals, yet to be individuals in community. This is the most perplexing problem of human existence to the person who has awakened to a religious level of existence; for, as Whitehead has said, the problem of religion is individuality in community.[3]

Man born into a community of other men has the dual responsibility of achieving an adequate subjective life, which centers in his sensory organism, and of growing into relations with his fellows. This is not one direction, but two; more so at some stages of his life than at others. The self-attentiveness that is required to fulfil the creatural possibilities of the subjective life may contribute to an accumulative intensification of the ego; yet to relax this self-attentiveness at this stage of growth, may mean the loss of capacity for qualitative meaning as an individual.

The advance toward the social orientation of the self requires some relinquishment of this self-atten-

[3] *Religion in the Making.* New York, Macmillan, 1926, p. 88.

tiveness. The Christian way of stating it is, the losing of one's life, which is a breaking down of egoistic barriers created by the emerging, subjective life.

In this transition from the fulfilment of spirit in the creation of the qualitative meaning of the individual, to the fulfilment of the spiritual relationship in community, there is something of a fusion of the aesthetic and ethical concerns. Kierkegaard represents the aesthetic interest and the ethical interest as "stages along life's way" and it is his contention that, as the individual matures, the aesthetic interest must give way to the ethical concern.[4] This is not satisfactory, it seems to me; for it leaves the spiritual import of the appreciative consciousness, in its creative effects upon the ethical consciousness, wholly uncalculated, and thus capitulates to an ethical criterion of life which does not take adequate account of the spiritual force of aesthetic values.

Here again, Whitehead seems to me to have been wiser than Kierkegaard, and wiser than most Christian theologians have been, when he insists that all order is aesthetic order, and the moral order is merely certain aspects of aesthetic order.[5] This at least implies that the ultimate fulfilment of any event, of any individual person, must be inclusive

---

[4] Soren Kierkegaard, *Stages Along Life's Way*. Princeton, Princeton University Press, 1940.

[5] A. N. Whitehead, *Religion in the Making*. New York, Macmillan, 1926.

of its diverse values and provide for their resolution in relationships.

If this analysis of the predicament of man's existence be true, the only way by which individual man can be redeemed from the threatening chaos of his own nature, is to be brought fully under the persuasion of this pattern-giving tenderness of God by which his being was created and by which his existence is also sustained. The imagery of the magnet is hard to resist here. Theologians have often employed it, notably Augustine, who likened Christ to an intruding magnet possessing the power of the Good, which came down into man's own orbit and attracted him into the orbit of God.

Not through sheer effortfulness in the pursuit of piety and strenuous good works, can our lives be redeemed from their chaos and darkness and ultimately turned toward the light; but through commitment to that tender working which is the Creative Source of all being, all goodness and beauty, all discrimination of truth and rightness, such that the sensibility in us can be magnified into dominance and made sovereign in our lives.

The lure of the Christ in this drama of redemption has always been that of the visible center of man's dedication—the incarnate one, the life possessed of the very conflicts of existence that make human nature distraught; yet objectified, oriented to the God of tenderness and strength, being himself, very God as tenderness and sacrificial love, working to redeem humankind. This has been the conviction.

In a way, one can say that the Christian drama of redemption revolves about the sense of form. Creation is the act of giving form to what is formless and void. Sin is the distortion of that formed in the image of God. Redemption is the recovery of form, through the return of these formless elements in the human chaos to a relationship with God that gives pattern and meaning to existence.

A most arresting critique of modern culture from the point of view of aesthetics has been recently made by Richard Hertz, author of *Man on a Rock,*[6] in *Chance and Symbol,* published by the University of Chicago Press. The root of our modern folly, according to this author, is in the loss of a sense of form and of symbol, resulting from our complete capitulation to the world of chance which knows nothing of history, nothing of the deep, persistent, and subtle stream of Process, as he calls it, out of which events emerge and by which they are conditioned. Being insensitive to the claims of form that arise from acquaintance with Process, the modern generation has become addicted to the praise of

[6] Chapel Hill, University of North Carolina Press, 1946.

power in naked form and to quantity which can also coerce. Power and number are the magic words of the unselective mentality, he argues, and breed a culture in which selectiveness becomes tabu.

This denial of a direction in life, indicated by form and idea, the author believes to be aesthetically unsound; but he advances this criticism as a spiritual judgment upon contemporary society. For him, aesthetics gives the clue to spiritual soundness, and on this ground, modern civilization is clearly unsound, he thinks. Therefore he states as a confession of faith that the current relinquishment of the restraint of form, giving way to the "pattern of impulse," or to sheer action and its consequent values, is a denial of what is basic in nature itself—a denial of the process that is history and the source of ourselves.

The solution of the modern problem, he insists, can be only one thing: namely, the relinquishment of our philosophy of chance with its idolatrous worship of power and number, and a return to the recognition of the redemptive power of symbol and form.

This may not seem altogether adequate to one for whom the spiritual concern goes beyond the problem of form and content. And the unrepentant liberal may be content to dismiss this analysis as the ranting of a disillusioned monarchist, pleading the lost cause of aristocracy, concluding that all that is involved in the cause of democracy and of humankind as democracy envisages it, stands repudiated by this aesthetic judgment. This conclusion would be unfair and superficial; and would overlook what is really a profound clue to our difficulty. We should not be insensitive to the redemptive power of form; for the curative implications are far-reaching. What the artist implies by form is not unrelated to what the theologian intends when he speaks of meaning in life—an organization of impulse and effort toward sovereign goals or ends such that some basis for discrimination, for acceptance and rejection, approval and judgment, for commitment and relinquishment, is made clear. The sense of value, whether religious or aesthetic, implies a sense of a sovereign good which restrains the egoistic impulse of both individual and culture, and turns life toward a higher dedication.

The theological way of achieving a sense of form in human life has been to view man's existence in relation to the demands of God, or in any case, to see this frail existence, so obviously transitory in its nature, in relation to what is ultimate and enduring.

But form is the exterior aspect of existence. The interior aspect is feeling. It is significant that form and feeling have been antithetical emphases in almost everything that man has created—in his art

and literature as well as in his religion. It is certainly
evident in Christianity. One can divide the denomi-
nations into exponents of form and the exponents
of feeling. This separation of form and feeling has
always been unfortunate, and it has had unfortunate
results in Christianity; for they really are inseparable facets of the creative life. Form without feeling
becomes sheer abstraction and ultimately degenerates into formalism; and feeling without a sense of
form becomes emotion without a disciplining structure, and degenerates into sentimentalism.

It is striking that Whitehead has built his entire
metaphysics around the elemental notion of feeling,
which he lifts to a creative principle in life that issues in structures of meaning and value. Thus, the
giving of tenderness to creation is, in this case, not
the sentimentalizing of existence, but the infusion
of feeling which becomes creative of form. The
form arises from the actualizing of relationships—
first in the creation of the individual's subjective
life, which is the drama of the individual life-span,
and second in the emergence of the objective relations by which individuals become aware of community; and ultimately, in the extension of these
objective relations to awareness of an ultimate concern, which is to complete the giving of pattern to
existence in relating men to God.

The story of creation, then, is the story of feeling

issuing into relationships, and of relationships creating a pattern of life, such that the values of feeling, the perceptions of beauty, of companionship, of goodness, the tendernesses of life, can be enjoyed and made to endure.

One may wonder what bearing all this talk about tenderness can have upon a world that is torn apart by industrial strife—a world facing revolution, possibly another war, and the imminence of atomic destruction.

I think it is terribly relevant. And I use the word *terribly* with more than its colloquial force. Our destiny hangs upon whether this Christian gospel of tenderness becomes creative of structures of consciousness which will turn the incalculable resources of pent-up power to meaningful and beneficent ends; or concern for this sensitive spirit languishes, enabling brute force to prevail, accelerating our chaos, and carrying us inevitably to destruction. At no time that any human being can imagine, has the concern for sensibility and discrimination been more relevant. At no time have the tendernesses of life which inhere in the Christian faith loomed more precious and real in their claim upon the human mind and heart.

I wonder if I might press this point more urgently. To speak of God's operations in history as a tender working is not to reduce it to sentiment which may or may not be ignored; it is rather to speak of it as a subtle, intricate, disciplined, restraining, resourceful, persistent, patient, and deep-working process, not unlike the skill of the artist hand, that shapes the crude clay into visible structures of beauty and intelligibility.

The power of this tender working is unique. The power that can transform sheer force into meaning and beauty, that can redeem tragedy, even transmuting tragic loss into blessedness, is a gentle might. This power can be measured only by such subtle means as are implied in the parables of Jesus. It is leaven, a seed, a hidden pearl of great price. Strength and sensitivity simultaneously operative, is the most apt figure for conceiving the nature of its working. The "love of a father" is a phrase which Christianity has used to express it—vigor combined with gentleness. "Faith that moves mountains," is another expression of it, faith that will cause the raging wind to cease, or that will call forth the merciless demon from the troubled brain of a lunatic child, and cure the child. These are all figures of speech in the teaching of Christianity which convey the sense of strength in these acts of tenderness in which blind force yields to the sensitive working of spirit.

His power lies in the fact that He, and He alone,

can give to every situation of actuality, intelligibility, beauty, and meaning. Cultures can ignore His tender working; men may flaunt their arrogance and proud intellects or wills; but they do so at the peril of inviting inescapable evil and destruction, by reason of the fact that without the dominance of this tender working, which gives order, restraint, resourcefulness to every actual occasion, the discipline and incentive to live meaningfully collapse.

This has become a reality to us in our time. The cultures of men, therefore, loom with new proportion and import of evil, when we view them in relation to this fact. Being constantly pressed into human assertiveness, without adequate recourse to sources of insight and direction, by which this human aggression might be sobered and related creatively to this working of God, the cultures of men mount with possibilities of violence, chaos, and destruction. These are always implicit in the actions of men because they are prone to construct society upon the short-sighted intentions and ends of human groups that leave the whole enterprise of God uncalculated.

For this reason, they who insist upon a sharp discontinuity between the concerns of God and the concerns of culture, seem justified. The contention that God and culture stand irreconcilably apart, however, overlooks profound and important aspects of the problem. In a way, sharp distinctions of this sort are oversimplifications. While the cultures of men may be said to remain powerful and potential obstructions to God's working, and tend to become aggressively hostile to His working by reason of their corporate arrogance, their autonomous pride, or simply their insensibility; this may be said only as a generalization on culture. It is somewhat in the form of an invective which sharpens up the enormity of man's corporate evil.

The concrete facts of the situation reveal subtle connections between God and culture by reason of the actualization of tenderness and sensitivity in specific human groups, in specific structures of human consciousness.

And the Lord said, If I find in Sodom fifty righteous within the city, then I will spare all the place for their sakes.[7]

And, as the story goes, God reduced the figure steadily until he declared to Abraham, "If there are ten righteous, I shall not destroy the city." This is an apt parable. Existence in most instances is sustained by a perilously slight margin of sensitivity. And the creative advance in any generation rests upon the responsiveness of a pitifully small margin

[7] *Genesis* 18:26.

of human consciousness. Yet it must be said that the degree of responsiveness in all individual lives, meager as it is, together with the responsiveness of the more dedicated lives, however small the proportion, provide structures of consciousness through which the tender working of God can influence the cultural experience toward value.

So long as concrete existence persists in any conscious human form, one would have to say that to that extent, connections between God's working and culture exist.

The salvation of a people has often depended upon a remnant; yet, salvation, even in these instances, would be impossible, were it not for the meager margin of sensitivity in the mass of mankind.

Analysis of man's corporate predicament reveals more clearly than any other kind of inquiry, how deeply man, in his collective life, is involved in conditions that oppose God's working; and yet, how indispensable, even in the autonomous society, this sensitive working is to man's bare existence, to say nothing of his redemption.

We understand our existence, then, when we understand its intent and when we discern the circumstances which condition our pursuit of that intent.

It has been my concern to point out in these lectures that the intent of our existence is given in the nature of creation itself—the creation of spirit out of process, which is the giving of sensitivity to force. I have ventured to illumine the psychical thrust that emerges in man as personal consciousness with the expectations of the Christian hope, and the Christian drama of redemption. While this must ultimately be embraced on faith, since anything beyond this sensory life-span must be so envisioned, yet it becomes congruous with a conception of life in which tenderness and the concern for meaning are sovereign over force.

But the intent of our being, so far as this visible span of years is concerned, is to be creative of spirit, which is to carry the intent of creation to such fulfilment as our structures of consciousness can achieve. Spirit is the qualitative meaning that emerges wherever the creative working of God is released in existence, such that feeling is actualized in meaningful form, meaning that God's spirit is imparted to existence.

The human enterprise is a spiritual enterprise when it has discerned this intent, and seeks, through redemptive means, to be restored by God's grace.

I submit that a renascent life of spirit could take hold of any generation of men and women for whom the concrete expressions of tenderness, beauty, and goodness were to become, not only the acknowledged ends of culture, but the moving forces in men's lives. Public education would find the imaginative arts as indispensable as the scientific and historical study of fact. Higher education would find ways of giving as much dedicated research and application to the development of discerning and spiritually motivated intellects as it has given to the development of the critical mind and the technician. The home would rediscover concern for sensibilities, and for the growth of the appreciative consciousness, such that an awakening of spirit in the child could emerge as a by-product of the family hearth. Religion would achieve a new maturity. Being sensible of the creative force of faith and of the sense of wonder, it, too, would rediscover the spiritual force of great music, great poetry and art, and bring these agencies of the human spirit into full use as a stimulus toward more daring imagination in the churches. Instead of sheer sentiment, divorced from discipline and intellectual intent, preaching and worship would come to depend upon such articulation of the inspired words of scripture and of the cultural tradition as would make knowledge and emotion one. The clarification of the human problem would mean illumination of facts in the light of a dedication. In this, the saint and the pure in heart would become our most practical realities, or at least comparable in esteem with the efficient and assertive leaders of society.

The concern for qualitative meaning, meaning that gathers into itself the rich fullness of relations, needs, and appreciations of a whole people, as when a community recalls its heritage, or contemplates the good of its common life, this concern for qualitative meaning would revolutionize our human mores, and establish new precedents for legislation and for community growth.

Let the vision become clear that God has created human beings to become structures of consciousness that will be creators and carriers of spirit, and in this, to glorify Him, and a new culture of the spirit will be forthcoming.

Being caught in the complexities of our own nature, we cannot readily rise to this intent. And thus the moral consciousness that keeps us alive to our limitations and warns us of judgment, is an indispensable aid. We shall never be completely freed from such demands as moral coercion may lay upon us. But our faith is impoverished, and the spiritual dimension of our culture is meager because we have been content to see religion as little more than an emotional assertion of the moral consciousness.

The fruition of the human spirit, and the completion of the Creator's intent in our lives, demands the development of an appreciative consciousness in people, in which the affections of men and women, their hungers and longings shall express the spiritual intent of their natures. Blessed are they who hunger and thirst after righteousness, for they shall be filled. This promise can be fulfilled only as the appreciation of spirit is awakened and the processes creative of good are made ample and operative in the institutions that nurture our lives.

The "good news of damnation" may arrest civilization's drift toward destruction. The good news of redemption points us to our intended destiny.